AGÜERO
GOAL KING

Trinity Mirror Sport Media

AGÜERO
GOAL KING

Copyright © Manchester City Football Club

The right of Manchester City Football Club to be identified as the owner of this work has been asserted in accordance with the Copyright, Designs and Patents Act, 1988.

All Rights Reserved. No part of this publication may be reproduced, stored in a retrieval system, or transmitted in any form, or by any means, electronic, mechanical, photocopying, recording or otherwise without the prior permission in writing of the copyright holders, nor be otherwise circulated in any form of binding or cover other than in which it is published and without a similar condition being imposed on the subsequent publisher.

Content Editor: David Clayton
Design: Rick Cooke, Colin Harrison
Jacket design: Rick Cooke
Sub-editors: Chris Brereton, James Cleary
Photography: Victoria Haydn, Tom Flathers, Sharon Latham, PA Images, Getty Images
Statistics: SAP
Thanks to: Will Beedles, Simon Heggie, Miles Gardiner, Paul Dove

First published in Great Britain and Ireland in 2017 by
Trinity Mirror Sport Media, PO Box 48, Old Hall Street, Liverpool, L69 3EB.

www.tmsportmedia.com
@SportMediaTM

Hardback ISBN: 9781910335963

Printed by Bell & Bain Ltd

CONTENTS

Sergio Aguero Interview — 08

Aguero Goal King

    2011/12 - AGUEROOOOO! — 16

    2012/13 - Becoming a Master — 54

    2013/14 - Mr Consistent — 78

    2014/15 - An Incredible Return — 116

    2015/16 - Simply Superb — 154

    2016/17 - The Record In Sight — 184

    2017/18 - A City Legend — 224

The Eric Brook Story — 236

Sergio's Statistics — 238

SERGIO INTERVIEW

THANK YOU

My life so far has passed very quickly and it doesn't seem five minutes since I was kicking a ball about in the back streets of the Quilmes neighbourhood in Argentina. So much has happened.

I started out when I was eight, made my senior debut aged 15 and when I turned 18, I went to Europe and signed for Atletico Madrid. In 2011, I joined City and now, here I am. My life in football has been something of a blur and the only thing I remember clearly from my younger years is that I just wanted to play football, nothing else. I didn't imagine or think about where I might end up, it was all about playing, playing, playing…

As a kid, I liked to think I was Michael Owen of Liverpool so they were the side I sort of followed in England. Owen and I were the same height more or less and I thought we had similar playing styles. My team in Argentina, Independiente, played in red, too. It's funny because everything was red back then! I liked River Plate, and when Enzo Francescoli was in the team, my dad drove me crazy talking about him. As I grew up, I started to understand the game better and I admired Javier Saviola and Carlitos Tevez – imagine how I felt when I became his teammate!

I always looked up to players with a similar style to mine and there were a lot of them – but I was playing football in the street all day, so I didn't have time to watch football matches that much; moreover, I think at that time we might not even have had a TV set to watch the game. When I was a kid, I never imagined I'd play in England one day and I didn't even think I'd play at the top level. When I first arrived at City, it was David Silva and Yaya Toure who helped me a lot. We just had to look at each other, no talking, and we got on with it. We kind of understood each other from the word go.

I remember Silva saying: 'Whenever I get the ball, you just run forward.' In the first two years, David and Yaya helped me a lot. Afterwards, the Club brought new signings in like Kevin De Bruyne, who is similar to David because he always tries to find me –

"My life in football has been something of a blur and the only thing I remember clearly from my younger years is that I just wanted to play football, nothing else. I didn't think about where I might end up, it was all about playing, playing, playing…"

SERGIO INTERVIEW

SERGIO INTERVIEW

the first thing he does is look up to see where I am or where I am moving to. I have to be even sharper these days because before it was David and Yaya with Yaya playing as holding midfielder, but now Kevin and David play in the same sort of role so I have to be doubly alert. And obviously, with our playing style these last two years, I have to look all around the pitch because we attack from any and every position. That is better for me, but still, David, Yaya and now Kevin, have been really important in helping me score goals.

When I scored my 178th goal for City against Napoli, I didn't even think I had broken the record! I just thought about winning that game. When I was about to shoot, I didn't think that goal would set a new record – I just focused on the game and afterwards, I realised what had happened and said to myself: 'Oh, finally!' After 78 years, I think it was about time the old record was broken.

It's something I'm going to better remember and look back on with pride when I retire and it will be then that I will probably realise better and think back to all the goals I scored here. However, if you think calmly, it's a crazy thing, it's a lot of years and I hope it lasts for many more now, although probably someone else will come up and take the record off me! So, I've broken the record, but life goes on and I will train every day and do my best in the next game and so on. I'm very happy and if I can keep scoring goals, so much the better, but winning as a team is the most important thing.

People have asked me what my idea is of the perfect goal. On one hand, the perfect goal for a player can be making it on his own, individually, while on the other hand, as a team it is much better to score after a good team play.

It's not important whether I get the goal or not, the key is the gameplay. It's different. In my opinion, it's more beautiful when you help create the chance yourself. That's when you don't depend on a cross, a pass or another player – it's you calling the shots, so it's more personal. I suppose examples would be the one I scored against QPR in 2012, or when we played Watford away during the 2017/18 season where I just got the ball and dribbled forward. The goal I scored against United at Old Trafford that proved to be the winner was special, too, when Yaya passed me the ball and I just thought of going forward, dribbling and trying to score. For a striker that's a perfect goal, but it is also great when you make it

Sergio is presented with the award for becoming City's all-time top goal scorer by Club Ambassador Mike Summerbee and Eric Brook's daughter, Betty Cougill, prior to the game against Arsenal on November 5, 2017

SERGIO INTERVIEW

"I love playing the Manchester derby against United - those are different games where to play beautiful football is not important anymore, it's all about winning"

after a team play. So, when I think about a really nice goal to score, I think about QPR and the day we won the title – I wish every goal could be like that!

Another question I'm sometimes asked is if I have a favourite team to play against or a favourite type of game? It depends on the match and, for me, there are two main categories – fiery games and open games.

I like playing against bigger teams because it is easier touching the ball all the time and you find and create more spaces than against other teams. I enjoy playing against Arsenal for instance, it's always a nice game, home and away and both teams try to play beautiful football. And, of course, I love playing the Manchester derby against United – those are different games where to play beautiful football is not important anymore, it's all about winning.

To finish, I'd like to thank a few people and dedicate my record to them.

First, I'd like to thank my teammates of today and to my former teammates who helped me, but have now left City. Gareth Barry, James Milner, Carlitos Tevez, Mario Balotelli... many of them from the first two or three seasons. And to Zaba, too – we shared some very nice moments at City.

Also, to the staff who work hard every day to help us recover from the games; for my family, my son and my agents who are all the time with me and my friends from Argentina as well.

But it's especially for the people that always supported me and for all the City fans who have been welcoming and warm towards me since I first arrived in Manchester. I thought at the beginning, the normal thing would've been to wait and see me play a couple of games to check whether I was good or not, but instead they trusted me from day one and I can't thank them enough for that.

So, there is still much to be done with City and there are possibilities spinning in my head every year. Of course, the main thing is winning titles and scoring goals – useful and historic – and someday I hope we can win the Champions League, too. My personal aim is to keep going, score more goals and win more titles with City. That will make me very happy and I hope it will make everyone else happy, too...

2011/12
SEASON

"I remember seeing the ball hitting the back of the net, hearing a deafening roar and things are hazy after that! I pulled off my shirt and wheeled away swirling it above my head as I went a little crazy. I knew that the time was up and that goal was going to win us the title but the shock didn't set in until my team-mates dragged me down on to the ground and started telling me they loved me"

48 GAMES
30 GOALS

GOAL KING

Off To A Flyer
v Swansea City 15.08.2011

Yaya Toure plays the ball to Micah Richards who races into the box before putting a low cross into the six-yard box and Aguero runs in to tap home at the far post. He was just nine minutes into his debut having come off the bench and the goal put City 2-0 up against the Swans. Three minutes later, an acrobatic flick set up David Silva to make it 3-0 and City fans quickly realised they were watching the debut of a very special player.

AGÜERO

90+1 mins

#2

Debut Double
v Swansea City 15.08.2011

What a way to start your life in sky blue. Already with a goal and an assist, Aguero collects the ball midway into the Swansea half and with little else on and time running out, he unleashes a sublime 25-yard shot that gives Swansea keeper Michel Vorm no chance and completes a 4-0 victory for the Blues. Two goals in just 33 minutes or so of first-team football for City – and he was in pain with blisters on his feet at the time, hence only being named a sub. The City fans had a new hero, but it was only the beginning…

#3

Pace And Power

v Tottenham Hotspur
28.08.2011

Samir Nasri plays a measured pass into the path of Aguero who picks up the ball on the left-hand side of the Spurs box. He drops his left shoulder and darts past defender Michael Dawson before thumping a left-foot shot high over Brad Friedel into the roof of the net for a superb individual effort that puts City 4-0 up at White Hart Lane. Explosive power, pace and strength – this goal has a bit of everything.

60 mins

AGÜERO

13 mins

#4

A Low Blow
v Wigan Athletic
10.09.2011

David Silva receives the ball on the left of the Wigan box and feigns a shot before looking up to see Aguero darting into the box. Kun takes the ball a touch to the right before hitting a low drive through the legs of a Wigan defender and into the bottom left-hand corner of the net to put City 1-0 up against the Latics.

GOAL KING

#5

Awesome Teamwork

v Wigan Athletic
10.09.2011

Sergio's second of the afternoon comes after a sublime team move. Yaya Toure plays a short pass to Silva who quickly flicks it to Nasri on the edge of the box. The midfielder just reaches the ball in time to nutmeg a defender as he passes into Aguero's path and the Argentine makes no mistake with a low shot past Ali Al-Habsi to double the Blues' lead.

63 mins

#6

Silva Lining
v Wigan Athletic
10.09.2011

This goal is created by the genius of Silva. The Spaniard picks up the ball on the halfway line and quickly has three Wigan players around him. A clever drag-back and piece of magic sees him wriggle free of his markers in a flash. He then spots Aguero's angled run in behind three Wigan defenders and plays a sublime pass through to leave Kun with enough time to size up the keeper and roll the ball past him into the corner of the net to make it 3-0. It was Sergio's fifth goal in 100 regulation minutes at the Etihad.

69 mins

AGÜERO

#7

Clinical At The Cottage
v Fulham 18.09.2011

Gareth Barry passes to Silva on the edge of the Fulham box and plays the ball through to Aguero who darts clear of his marker before drawing Mark Schwarzer off his line and tucking the ball over the keeper and into the corner of the net to give City the lead at Craven Cottage.

18 mins

GOAL KING

#8

Double Delight

v Fulham 18.09.2011

Edin Dzeko leaps to head down a long ball forward into the path of Aguero. In a flash, the Argentina star takes one touch before firing a low shot from 20 yards out that arrows into the bottom corner past Schwarzer to double City's lead.

AGÜERO

90+3 mins

GOAL KING

#9

Leaving It Late
v Villarreal 18.10.2011

With City being held at home to Villarreal in the Champions League and time running out, the Blues launch one last, hopeful attack. Pablo Zabaleta crosses low into the six-yard box and Silva's extravagant back-flick sees the ball head towards the far post where Aguero lunges just ahead of Dzeko to bundle the ball over the line for a dramatic, last-gasp winner.

AGÜERO

69 mins

#10

Bragging Rights

v Manchester United
23.10.2011

A forward pass finds Mario Balotelli who back-flicks the ball to James Milner. Milner spots Micah Richards' burst down the right flank and the City defender sends a low ball into the six-yard box that Aguero simply wants more. It is his boot that connects first to put the Blues 3-0 up and well on the way to a biggest win at Old Trafford since 1926.

GOAL KING

#11

A Spot-kick Master
v Newcastle United
19.11.2011

When Micah Richards is felled in the box by Hatem Ben Arfa, Sergio collects the ball and places it on the spot. Mario Balotelli had already scored a penalty earlier in the game but had been substituted, so Aguero steps up and calmly slots the ball to Tim Krul's left to put City 3-0 up against the previously unbeaten Magpies.

72 mins

AGÜERO

#12

Ending The Pain
v Arsenal
29.11.2011

City hadn't won away to Arsenal for 36 years, but Aguero's late goal puts an end to the long barren run. With the score 0-0 in this League Cup quarter-final at the Emirates, Edin Dzeko's excellent run and cross-field pass eventually finds its way to Aguero who nudges the ball forward before he rifles a low shot past Lukasz Fabianski into the bottom corner to send the Blues into the semi-finals.

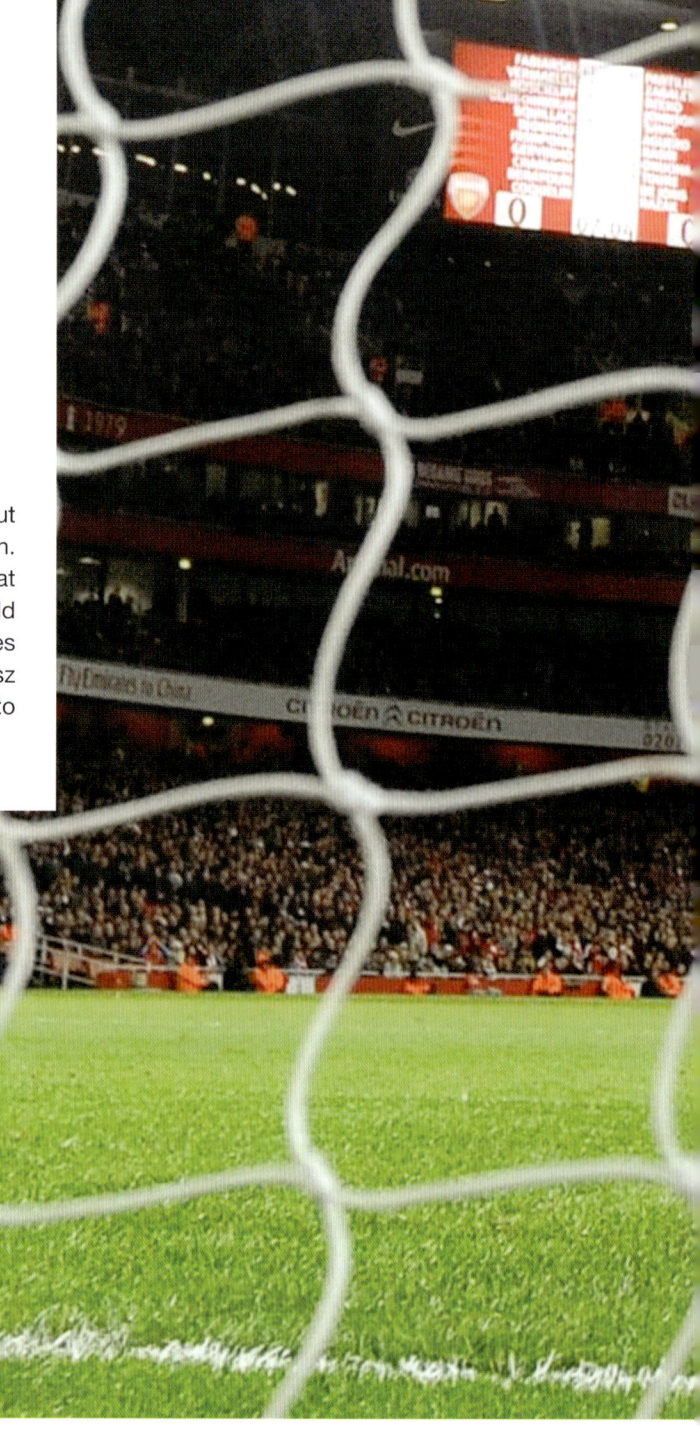

GOAL KING

83 mins

AGÜERO

32 mins

#13

Simply Unbelievable
v Norwich City 03.12.2011

This was a goal that almost had to be seen to be believed. Micah Richards' burst into the box sees the right-back squeeze a cross into the feet of Aguero. With five players surrounding him he drops his shoulder to go one way, putting two defenders off balance before toe-poking the ball home from six yards through a proverbial forest of legs to give the Blues the lead.

29 mins

#14

Easy Pickings
v Stoke City
21.12.2011

The scrappiest goal so far. Yaya Toure hits a low shot that Vincent Kompany turns goalwards but keeper Thomas Sorensen parries the shot across goal to the lurking Aguero who has the simplest of tasks to tap into the empty net to put City ahead.

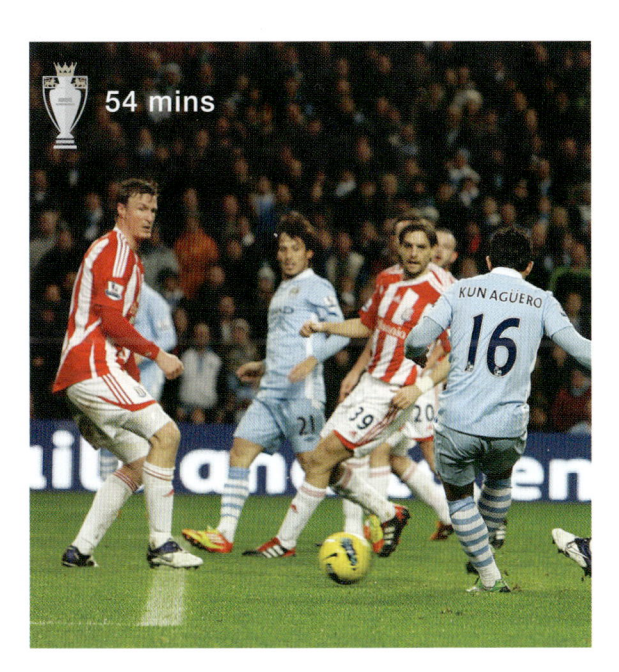

54 mins

#15

Merry Christmas
v Stoke City
21.12.2011

Sergio's second of the afternoon and City's third on the night, this was another clinical finish from close range. Gareth Barry finds Samir Nasri who plays a slide-rule ball across the box, flat-footing two Stoke defenders before Aguero tucks home from six yards out to ensure City top the Premier League table at Christmas.

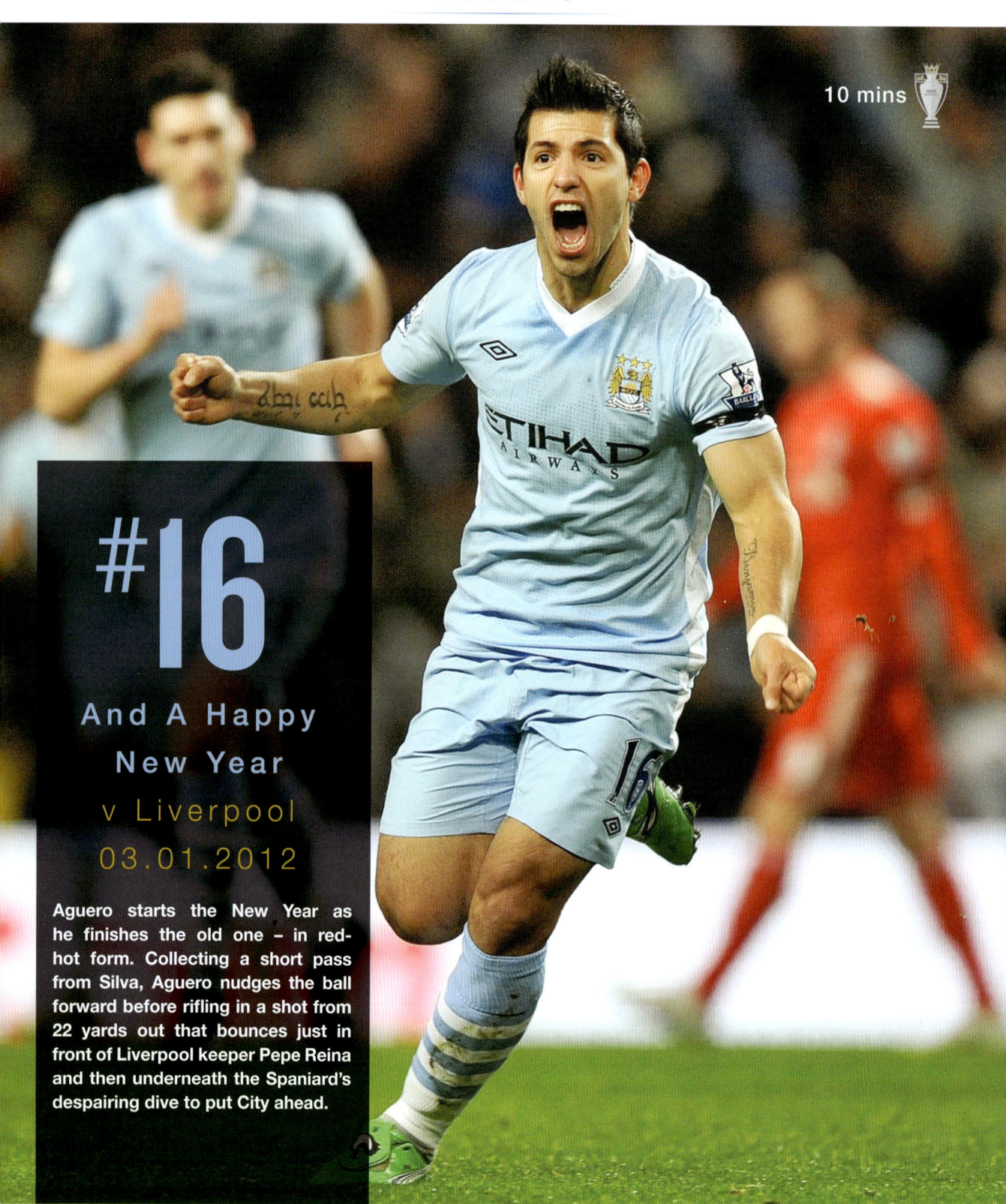

AGÜERO

10 mins

#16

And A Happy New Year

v Liverpool
03.01.2012

Aguero starts the New Year as he finishes the old one – in red-hot form. Collecting a short pass from Silva, Aguero nudges the ball forward before rifling in a shot from 22 yards out that bounces just in front of Liverpool keeper Pepe Reina and then underneath the Spaniard's despairing dive to put City ahead.

GOAL KING

#17

Fighting Back
v Manchester United
08.01.2012

City had fallen 3-0 behind by the break against United, just two months after thrashing the Reds 6-1 at Old Trafford. City fans fear the worst but Aleks Kolarov pulls one back early in the second half and just past the hour Aguero meets a low cross on the full that David De Gea manages to keep out, but Kun is first to the loose ball and he makes no mistake from close range.

64 mins

AGÜERO

10 mins

#18

Ice Cool

v Fulham

04.02.2012

As Manchester is gripped by blizzard conditions, so City sweep Fulham away with a bright and breezy start. The Blues are ahead after just 10 minutes as Aguero bags only his second penalty for the Club. He sends Mark Schwarzer the wrong way from the spot as City go on to win 3-0 at the Etihad.

#19

Super Sub
v FC Porto
16.02.2012

With the clock running down and City drawing 1-1 in the Europa League first leg against FC Porto, second-half sub Sergio arrived to swing the tie City's way. In a move that starts with Yaya Toure and Samir Nasri playing a one-two, the Ivorian powers into the box before squaring the ball for Aguero to tap home from six yards out.

84 mins

AGÜERO

1 min

GOAL KING

#20

Fast Forward

v FC Porto

22.02.2012

His fastest goal so far! Porto lose possession and the ball falls to Yaya Toure who plays a pass into Aguero's path. The City striker runs into the box before a low, right-foot shot into the bottom corner gives the Blues an early lead and the first goal of what turns out to be a comfortable 4-0 win at the Etihad.

AGÜERO

52 mins

#21

Right Place, Right Time
v Blackburn Rovers 25.02.2012

Another poacher's goal. A corner on the right is swung in by David Silva, Blackburn keeper Paul Robinson flaps at the cross and palms the ball down to Aguero who lashes it back past the former England keeper from eight yards to double City's lead on the day.

GOAL KING

#22
Providing Hope
v Sporting Lisbon
15.03.2012

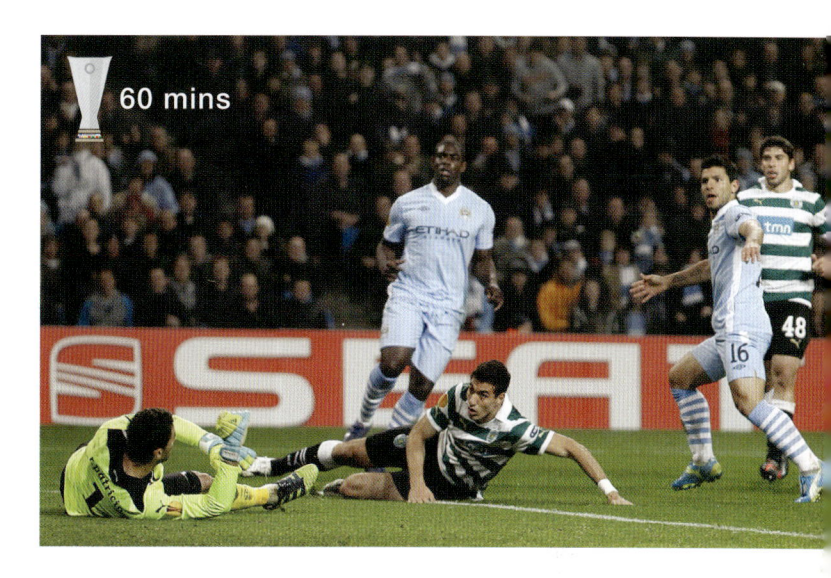

City have surprisingly fallen 2-0 down to Sporting Lisbon in the Europa League Round of 16 second leg. Already trailing 1-0 from the first leg, the Blues look down and out until Yaya Toure spots Aguero in space in the Lisbon box. He plays a short pass to his feet, the Argentine swings his right foot at the ball and sends a shot which gives Rui Patricio no chance.

60 mins

#23
Grandstand
v Sporting Lisbon
15.03.2012

This goal sets up a grandstand finish as City come from 2-0 down to lead 3-2 on the night, level the aggregate scores at 3-3 but still trail on the away goals rule. Aleks Kolarov's corner finds the head of Edin Dzeko who gets enough contact to divert the ball towards the lurking Aguero who hooks a volley in from close range to put the Blues ahead. But for a great late save, Joe Hart's header comes within a whisker of winning the game for City who eventually run out of time and exit the competition a few seconds later.

82 mins

AGÜERO

78 mins

GOAL KING

#24

Staying On Track

v Chelsea

21.03.2012

With City desperate to close the gap on leaders United, losing at home to Chelsea isn't any option. Yet with time running out, Gary Cahill's goal on the hour-mark separates the teams. Then, Pablo Zabaleta's shot is handled in the box by Michael Essien and Aguero steps up to calmly slot home his 24th goal of the season and put the Blues level before Samir Nasri's late winner keeps City's title ambitions on track.

AGÜERO

6 mins

#25

Keeping The Pressure On
v West Bromwich Albion 11.04.2012

With City and United both in action in midweek, the Blues need to keep winning games and hope the Reds slip up. Sergio ensures this game gets off to a flying start as he picks the ball up just inside his own half, skips past a couple of challenges and then lashes a 25-yard shot past Ben Foster to put the Blues in front.

GOAL KING

#26

A Night To Remember
v West Bromwich Albion
11.04.2012

As news filters through that United have gone behind to Wigan Athletic, Samir Nasri feeds a pass through to David Silva in the West Brom penalty area but it's Sergio who arrives first, steering an angled shot past Foster for his second of the night as the Blues claw back three points from United's lead in a pivotal night of the 2011/12 title race.

54 mins

AGÜERO

#27

Unstoppable
v Norwich City
14.04.2012

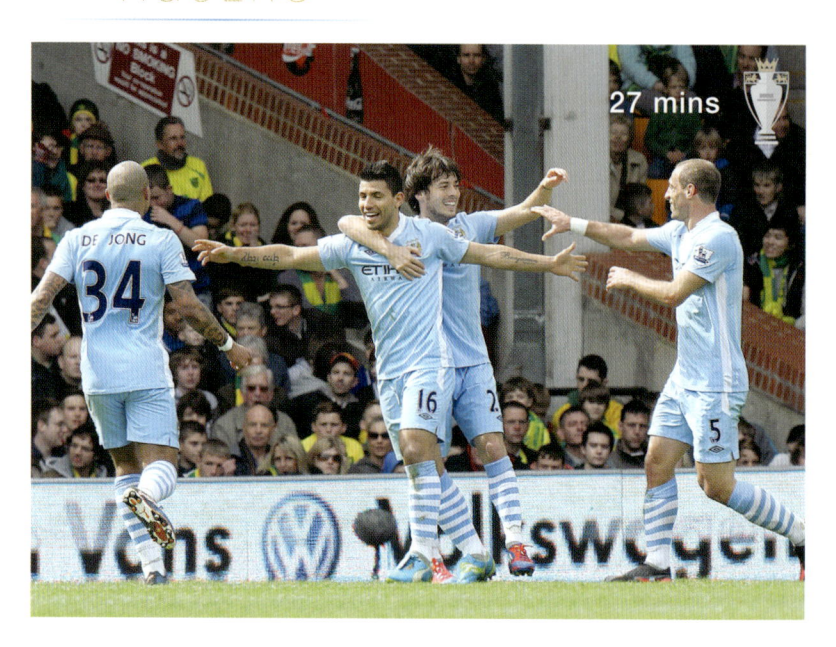

27 mins

An absolute beauty. Aguero heads towards the Norwich box and plays a short pass to Carlos Tevez who back-heels the ball into Sergio's path and he thunders and unstoppable shot from 18 yards out, high into the top left-hand corner to give keeper John Ruddy no chance and double the Blues' lead.

75 mins

#28

Back For More
v Norwich City
14.04.2012

Sergio's second of the afternoon comes as he carries the ball into the Norwich box before cutting inside and lifting a clever shot over the diving Ruddy into the far corner as the Blues head for a second 6-1 win on the road this campaign.

GOAL KING

27 mins

#29

The Race Gets Tighter
v Wolverhampton Wanderers 22.04.2012

Relegation-threatened Wolves resist for as long as they can but finally, City break the deadlock. Gael Clichy's excellent ball puts Aguero clear in the box and though he begins to stumble as the keeper comes towards him, he still has the nous to poke the ball past him and into the net from close range.

AGÜERO

GOAL KING

90+4 mins

#30

A Moment In History
v Queens Park Rangers
13.05.2012

It's doubtful Sergio will ever score a more memorable or important goal as the one he did on 13 May 2012. City, needing a win to secure a first top-flight title for 44 years, trail 2-1 to QPR with just added time remaining, but when Edin Dzeko's header levels the scores, there's still time for one last attack. Aguero comes into midfield, looking for the ball and Nigel de Jong plays it to him. Knowing this could be the last chance, he plays it into the feet of Mario Balotelli who holds off a challenge and returns the ball as he starts to stumble. Sergio takes it into the box, skips past one challenge and then fires a low shot past Paddy Kenny to spark scenes of wild celebrations at the Etihad. His 30th goal of an incredible first campaign in England and it just happens to be the title winner, too!

2012/13
SEASON

"The second season was always going to be difficult after the emotion of the previous campaign. As the 2011/12 season had progressed, teams began to play us in a different, more cautious way. I think we caught a lot of teams by surprise in our title-winning season because nobody was that aware of us or what we were capable of"

40 GAMES
17 GOALS

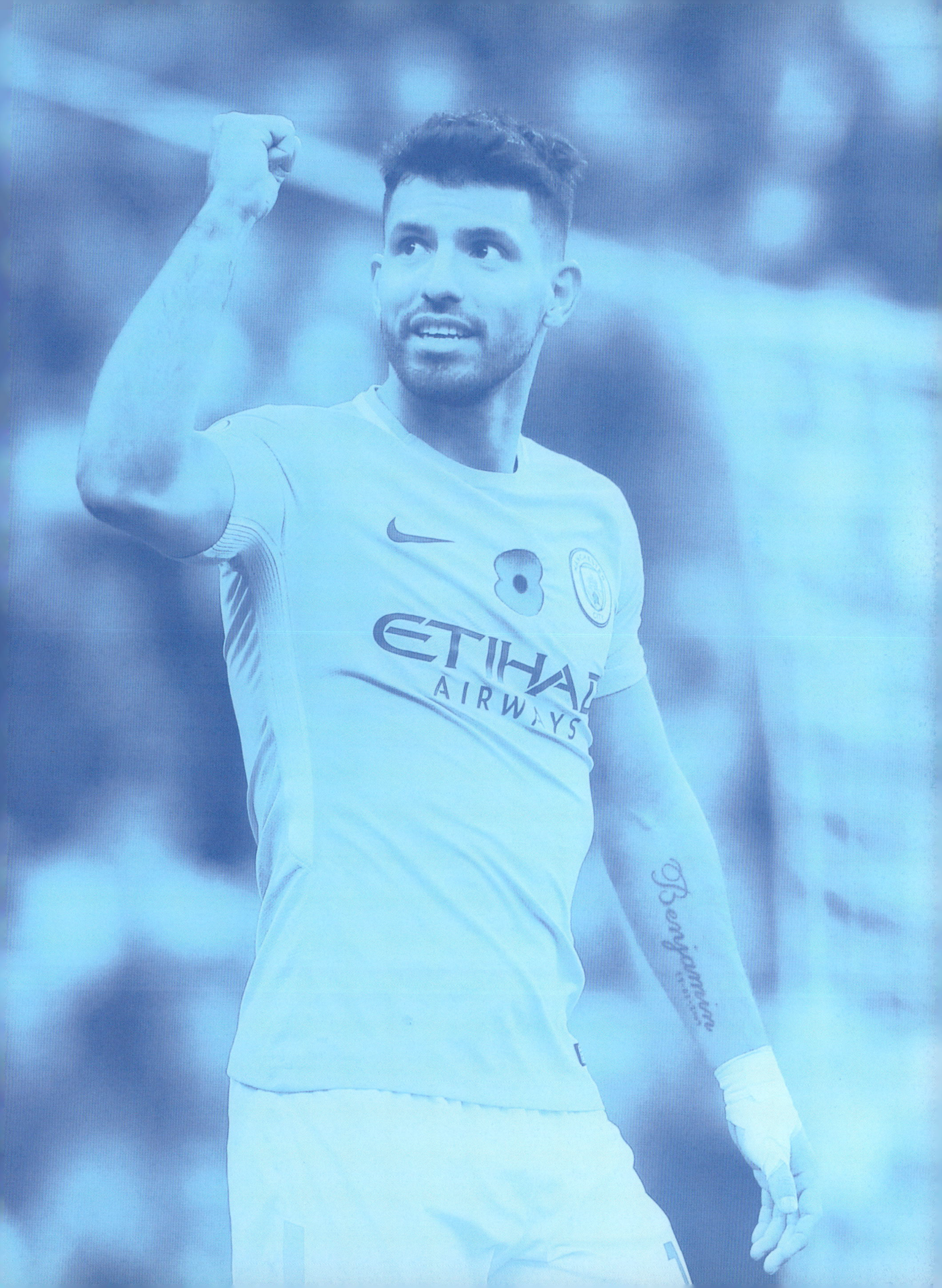
AIRWAYS

AGÜERO

43 mins

#31

New Season, Same Story
v Fulham 29.09.2012

Sergio's first of the new season comes as Carlos Tevez fires a shot in that is guided goalwards by David Silva, only for Mark Schwarzer to make an amazing save – but Aguero is first to the loose ball and he has the easiest of tap-ins from two yards to get his season up and running almost two months into the campaign.

GOAL KING

#32

Perfect Timing

v Sunderland
06.10.2012

David Silva starts the move that leads to the Blues doubling their lead against Sunderland. The Spaniard plays a pass to Aleks Kolarov on the left flank and the Serbian fires in a low cross that Aguero runs on to and lashes home from six yards out with perfect timing.

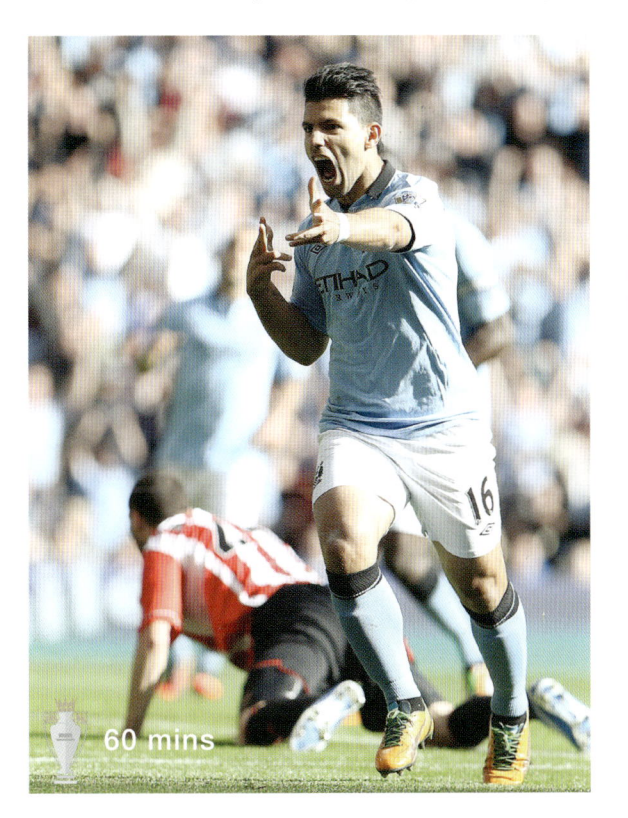

74 mins

#33

Super Mario

v Ajax
06.11.2012

City have fallen 2-0 behind in their Champions League group clash with Ajax but having halved the deficit, a long clearance forward finds the head of Mario Balotelli. He nods the ball on and into the path of Aguero who takes a couple of paces before firing a low shot across the keeper and into the bottom left-hand corner from the edge of the box.

60 mins

#34

Beautifully Done
v Tottenham Hotspur
11.11.2012

Trailing 1-0 to Spurs, City need inspiration to get back into the game – and it comes, just past the hour-mark. Carlos Tevez's attempted pass is cut out but Yaya Toure quickly wins back possession and diverts the ball into Aguero's path – he cuts the ball back inside as he heads into the box before expertly guiding a left-foot shot past the keeper to level the scores.

65 min

54 mins

#35

A Cool Conversion

v Aston Villa 17.11.2012

A controversial penalty after the referee awards the spot-kick for handball following David Silva's corner. Sergio coolly converts with a low shot past the keeper to double City's lead on the day.

GOAL KING

#36

Power Serge
v Aston Villa
17.11.2012

If his first goal had been somewhat fortuitous, Kun's second is excellent. Picking up the ball on the right, he drifts into the Villa penalty area before dropping his shoulder past the defender. He then fires a low shot under the keeper as City go on to win 5-0.

67 mins

AGÜERO

#37

Real Deal
v Real Madrid
21.11.2012

Aguero wins and converts the penalty that draws City level with Real Madrid. After being fouled in the box, Kun sends the keeper the wrong way from the spot but the draw isn't enough for the Blues who are eliminated from the competition as a result.

GOAL KING

73 mins

10 mins

#38

Early Xmas Present
v Newcastle United
15.12.2012

City go in front after only 10 minutes with a move that begins with Yaya Toure's through-ball to Samir Nasri and the Frenchman's unselfish side pass to Aguero gives the Argentina striker an easy chance to convert from seven yards out.

AGÜERO

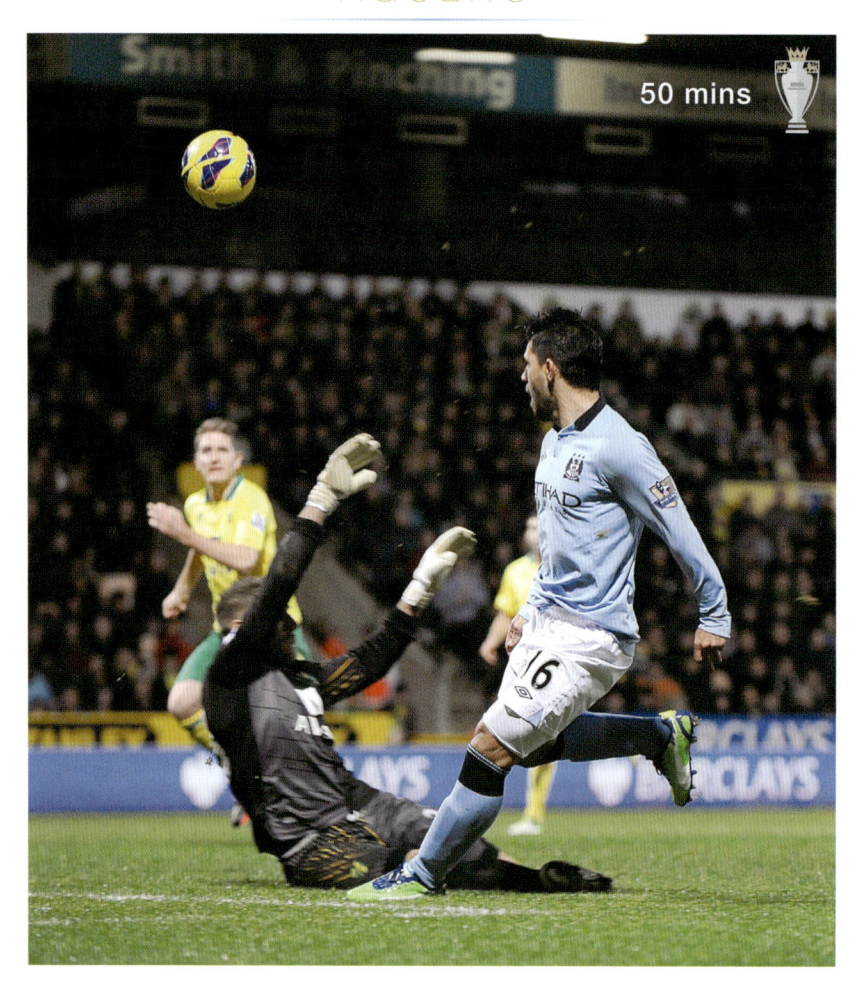

#39

Canaries Clipped

v Norwich City 29.12.2012

City start like a house on fire with Edin Dzeko scoring twice in the first four minutes, but when Samir Nasri is sent off later in the half and the hosts reduce the deficit, it looks like being a long afternoon for the Blues. But Yaya Toure's vision sets free Aguero who holds off the challenge of Sebastian Bassong to lift the ball over the keeper and restore City's two-goal advantage.

GOAL KING

#40

Double Figures
v Stoke City
01.01.2013

City were already two goals ahead against a Stoke side that had arrived at the Etihad on the back of an unbeaten 10-game run. Pablo Zabaleta and Edin Dzeko give the Blues the lead before David Silva is hauled down on the edge of the box, the referee points to the spot and Aguero calmly slots home his 10th of the campaign.

74 mins

AGÜERO

78 mins

#41

One Of The Best

v Liverpool
03.02.2012

This is one of Sergio's best goals for the Blues and it is just a pity it isn't the winner as it was worthy of settling any game. City led, but Liverpool come back to lead 2-1 and when Aguero chases a hopeful ball towards the Liverpool corner flag, there is little on. But Pepe Reina's rash decision to chase the ball sees Kun nudge it past the Reds' keeper and pivot a shot from a seemingly impossible angle in off the underside of the crossbar to earn City a 2-2 draw.

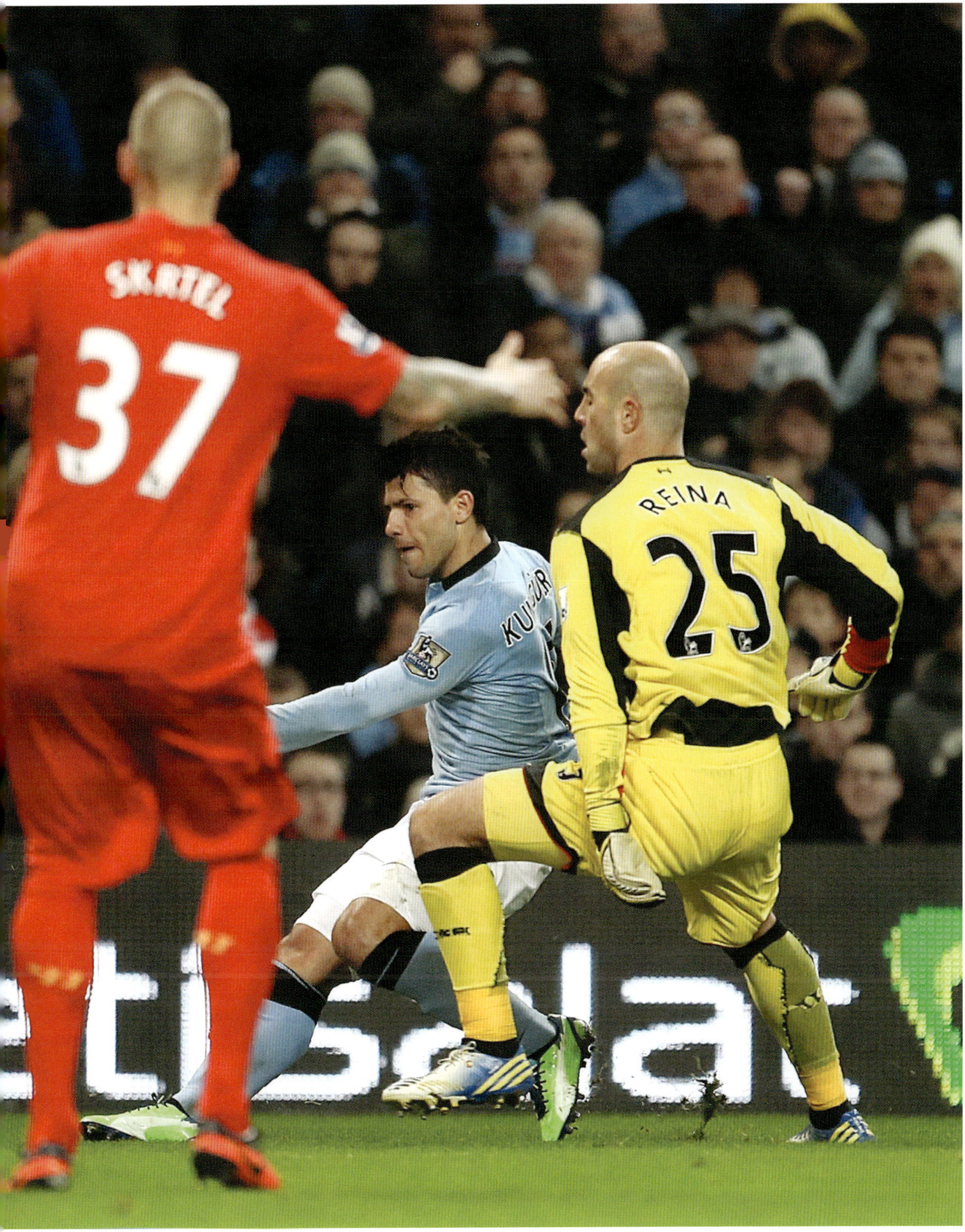
SKRTEL
37
REINA
25

AGÜERO

15 mins

#42

Unstoppable
v Leeds United
17.02.2013

Another penalty dispatched by Sergio who is fouled in the box and delivers maximum punishment himself from the spot with a customary cool finish.

GOAL KING

#43

Silva Platter
v Leeds United
17.02.2013

Kun's second of the afternoon comes courtesy of a superb piece of vision by David Silva. The playmaker holds the ball up on the right before lofting a clever ball over the Leeds defence for Aguero to run on to and finish with a low shot off the post to complete a 4-0 rout for the Blues.

74 mins

AGÜERO

78 mins

GOAL KING

#44

Blue Swoon
v Manchester United
08.04.2013

This was a stunning goal that was all about the power and strength Aguero possesses. With the scores level at Old Trafford, Aguero picks up the ball outside the United box, powers past four challenges before sending an arrowed shot into the top corner from the edge of the six-yard box to secure another memorable Old Trafford victory and send the travelling City fans wild.

#45

First Time For Everything
v Chelsea
14.04.2013

A first for Sergio – a header – and a goal worthy of this FA Cup semi-final at Wembley. City are 1-0 up and the second period has just restarted when Gareth Barry lofts a tempting cross into the Chelsea box for Aguero to leap highest and send a looping header past Petr Cech – all-but securing the Blues' place in the FA Cup final for the second time in three years.

47 mins

AGÜERO

28 mins

#46

Finishing Strong

v West Ham United 27.04.2013

City have long accepted the title will3 not be coming back to the Etihad for a second successive season but still want to finish the campaign on a high. West Ham defend well in the opening stages but Samir Nasri's dart to the bye-line and low cross gives Aguero a clear sight of goal and he makes no mistake with a left-foot shot from six yards out.

GOAL KING

#47

Well Read
v Reading
14.05.2013

City's first game following the dismissal of manager Roberto Mancini is away to Reading – but Sergio continues his fine run in sky blue with the opening goal of the game on 40 minutes. The result of a delightful triangular passing move, David Silva and James Milner combine with the latter's low cross turned in by Aguero with a smart right-foot finish from close range – his 17th and final goal of his second season at the Club.

40 mins

2013/14
SEASON

"I didn't score – it wasn't really my day in front of goal – but it was a privilege to be part of the occasion. Our second title in three years – it was very satisfying and I'm happy to have played my part, even though I was forced to miss much of the second part of the season"

34 GAMES
28 GOALS

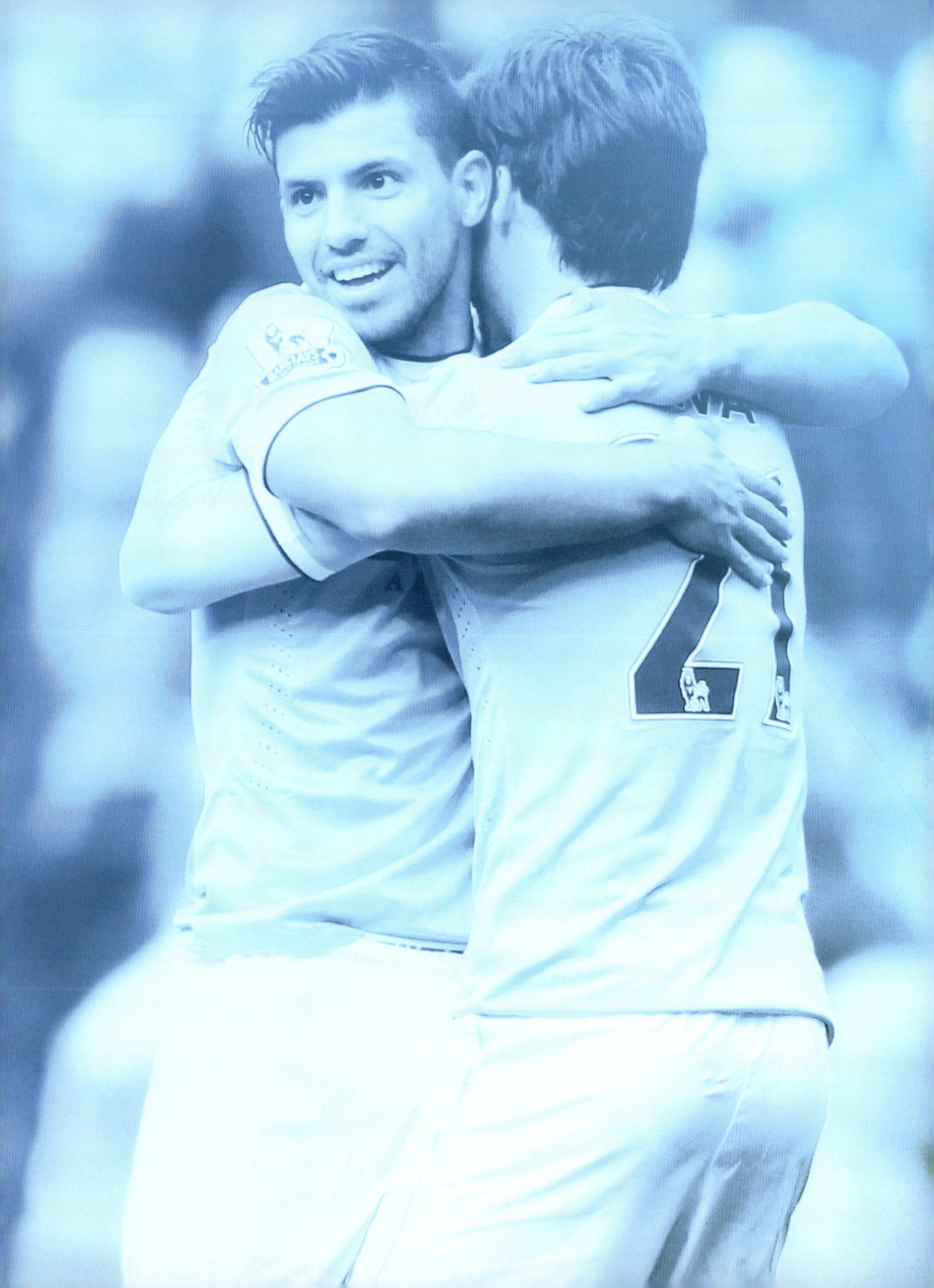

AGÜERO

#48

Calling The Toon

v Newcastle
19.08.2013

It takes Sergio just 22 minutes of Manuel Pellegrini's reign to find the back of the net as the Blues start the 2013/14 campaign in rip-roaring fashion. Aguero collects the ball in midfield before turning on the afterburners. He then fires a low shot into the bottom left-hand corner from 20 yards – a terrific way to start the new season.

GOAL KING

22 mins

AGÜERO

58 mins

#49

Left Or Right
v Viktoria Plzen
17.09.2013

Proof, if it were needed, that Kun is lethal with either foot comes when he sweeps home a Champions League goal in the Czech Republic. Samir Nasri plays in a short pass to Aguero in the box and, with his back to goal, he initially nudges the ball forwards before turning and lashing in a low left-foot shot with typical accuracy.

GOAL KING

#50

Plenty More To Come

v Manchester United
22.09.2013

What a way for City's No.16 to bring up his 50th goal – in the 16th-minute of course! Samir Nasri's flick to Aleks Kolarov sees the Serbian power the ball into the six-yard box where Aguero reacts in an instant, hooking a left-foot volley past David De Gea to put the Blues on the way to another Manchester derby win. Clinical, instinctive and sublime – this landmark strike has everything.

16 mins

AGÜERO

47 mins

GOAL KING

#51

Blues Go Wild

v Manchester United

22.09.2013

What better way to celebrate reaching the 50-goal mark than to start your next half-century? City increase the lead over United with a goal that highlights United's defensive frailties as Aguero is again allowed too much space and time to score his second of the afternoon. The creator this time is Alvaro Negredo who is able to turn easily just inside the box. He whips in a cross that Sergio volleys with enough power to beat David De Gea for the second time in a little over half-an-hour as the rampant Blues open up a three-goal lead.

AGÜERO

45 mins

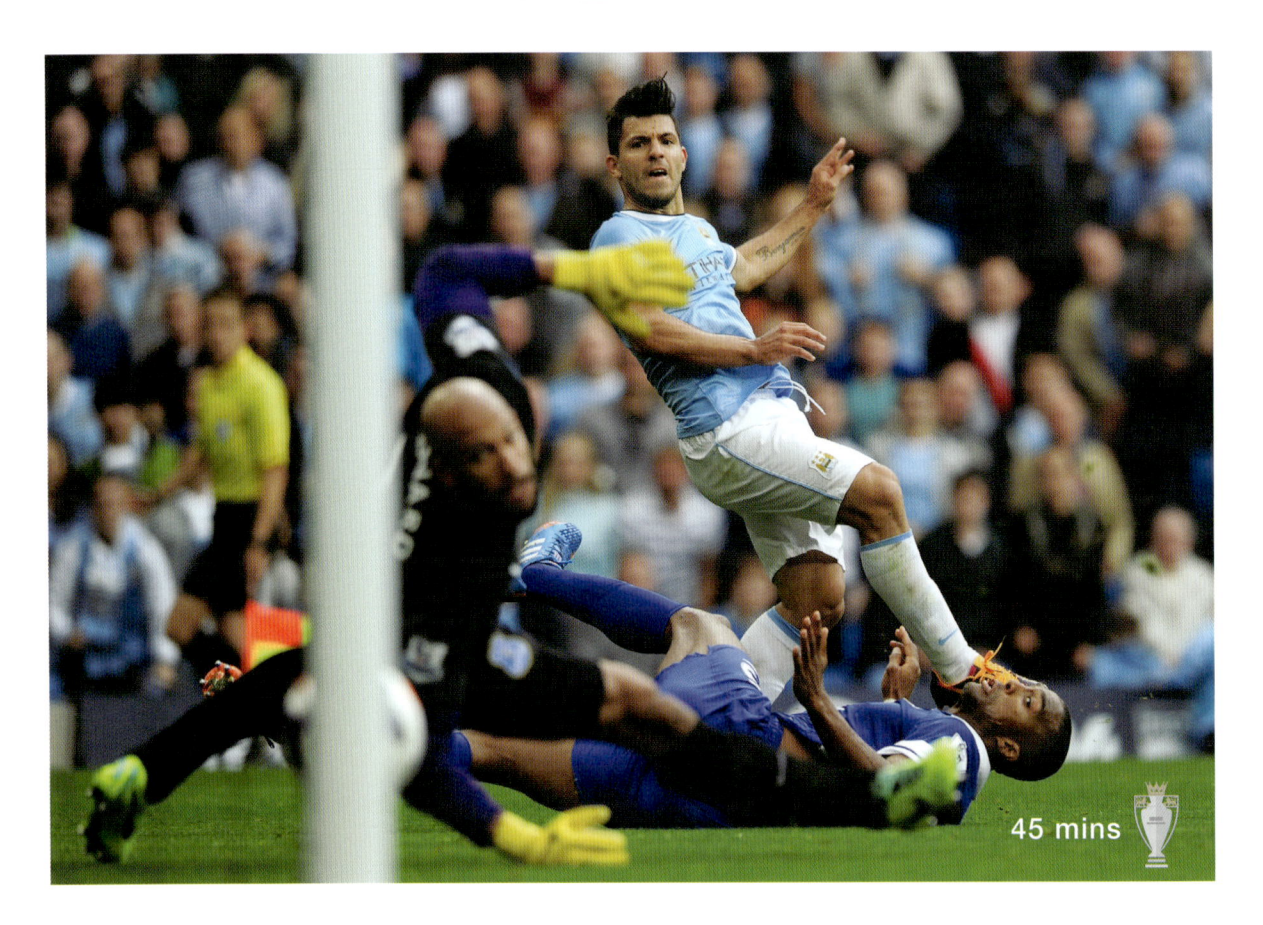

#52

No Second Chances
v Everton 05.10.2013

A goal made by the vision of David Silva and finished by the excellence of Sergio Aguero. There seems to be little on as Silva drives forward towards the Everton box then, as Aguero makes a clever dart to the right, Silva looks as though he will play it to his left before playing a pass into Kun's path and his first-time angled shot gives Toffees keeper Tim Howard no chance on his near post. Clinical.

GOAL KING

#53

Upton Spark
v West Ham United 19.10.2013

Fernandinho's pass to Alvaro Negredo sees the Spaniard leave the ball for Sergio who bursts through the West Ham defence, draws the keeper off his line and then tucks the ball into the bottom left-hand corner to give City the lead at Upton Park.

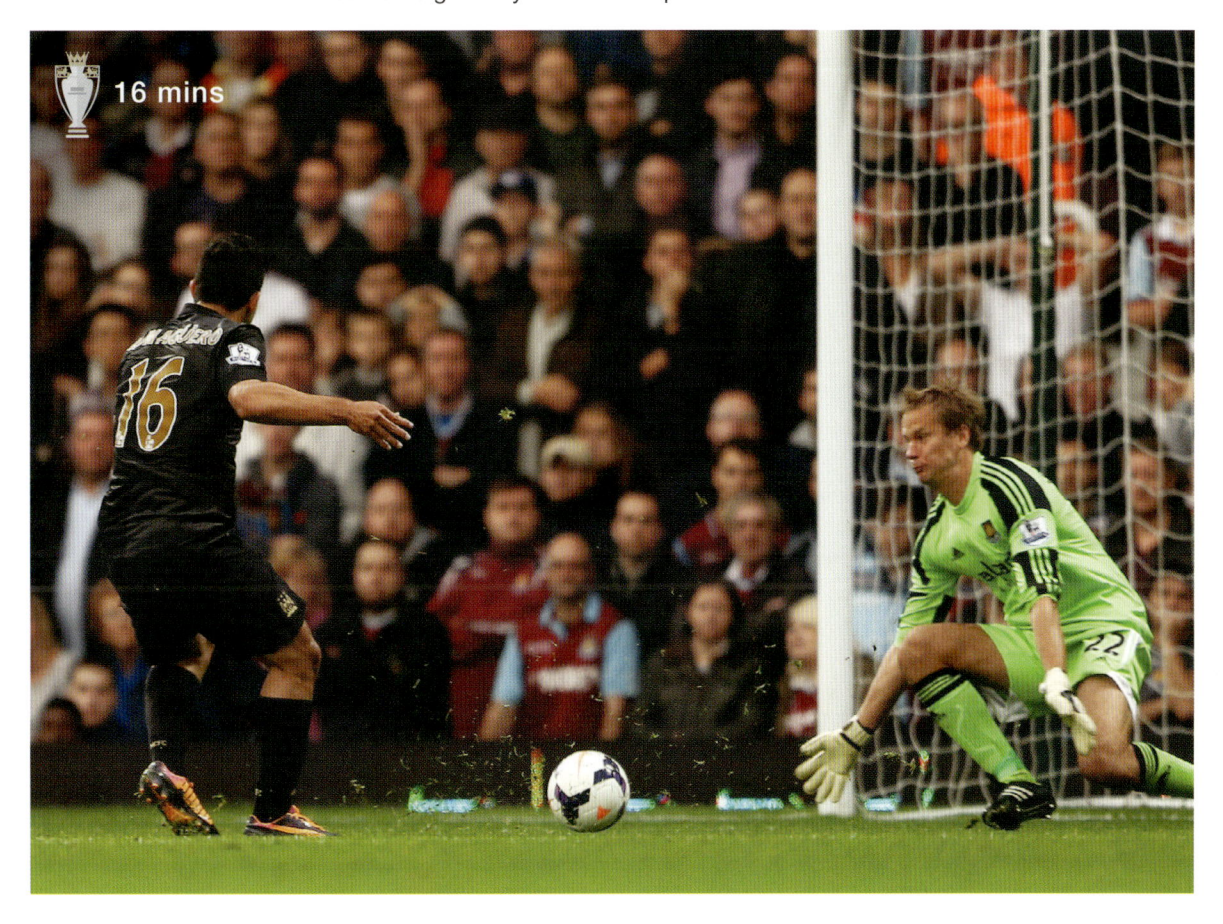

16 mins

AGÜERO

#54

Making It Look Easy

v West Ham United

19.10.2013

Sergio's second of the game against West Ham comes six minutes into the second-half as he heads home David Silva's free-kick from the right with ease thanks to some woeful marking by the home defence.

GOAL KING

51 mins

AGÜERO

#55

Yet Another Brace
v CSKA Moscow
23.10.2013

The first of another brace for Sergio, David Silva races into the CSKA box on the left before picking out Aguero's run – he just nips in ahead of the defender and then slots it to the goalkeeper's left to put City level just two minutes after falling behind.

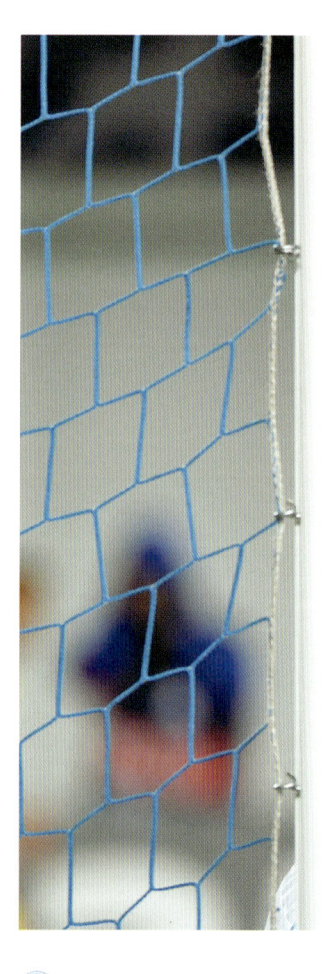

34 mins

GOAL KING

42 mins

#56

Heads Up
v CSKA Moscow
23.10.2013

Another header! This time the cross is supplied by Alvaro Negredo who digs out a clever cross just inside the CSKA box and Aguero bravely arrives just before the goalkeeper to head home from close range and put City on the way to a vital 2-1 away win in Russia.

AGÜERO

#57

Wrong But Right

v Chelsea

27.10.2013

As good as any goal you're likely to see considering it was his 'wrong' foot. City are trailing 1-0 when Samir Nasri nudges the ball into Aguero's path and in a flash, the Argentina star rifles a left-foot shot high into the top left-hand corner to level the scores at Stamford Bridge – a fantastic goal.

GOAL KING

49 mins

AGÜERO

#58

Clinical
v Norwich City
02.11.2013

David Silva's low ball from the left is only half-cleared by the Norwich City defence and Aguero is on hand to lash the ball home from eight yards.

71 mins

3 mins

#59

Record Breaker
v CSKA Moscow 05.11.2013

After David Silva is fouled in the box, Sergio steps forward to hammer home the resulting penalty to give City the lead and become the Blues' top scorer in European competition at the same time.

GOAL KING

20 mins

#60

Conjured Class
v CSKA Moscow
05.11.2013

Another goal out of nothing. Samir Nasri's arrowed pass finds Sergio in the box with his back to goal, but he spins away from his marker and fires into the bottom right-hand corner with a shot across the keeper to double the Blues' lead on the night.

AGÜERO

41 mins

GOAL KING

#61

Nicely Done

v Tottenham Hotspur

24.11.2013

The first of another brace of goals, Jesus Navas scampers down the right before whipping a ball into the six-yard box for Aguero to open his body and guide the ball past Hugo Lloris with a deft left-foot finish.

AGÜERO

50 mins

GOAL KING

#62

Cruise Control
v Tottenham Hotspur 24.11.2013

Sergio's second of the game and the Blues' fourth of the afternoon was a goal made by Yaya Toure. The Ivory Coast midfielder bursts into the box before squaring a pass at speed to Aguero who side-foots home with aplomb from eight yards out.

AGÜERO

#63

No Mistake
v Viktoria Plzen
27.11.2013

Sergio is fouled as he crosses the ball into the Plzen box and a penalty is awarded by the referee. Kun dusts himself down to take the penalty and he makes no mistake from the spot as he sends the keeper the wrong way with a low shot to the left.

33 mins

GOAL KING

9 mins

#64

Bagging At The Baggies
v West Bromwich Albion
04.12.2013

A lovely move starts with Edin Dzeko playing a clever ball inside the full-back for Pablo Zabaleta to run on to. The City defender then spots Aguero in the box and plays a low cross in at pace and Aguero fires home from close range for a goal made in Argentina!

AGÜERO

#65

Neat And Tidy
v Southampton
07.12.2013

A good run and cross by Aleks Kolarov sees the Serbian left-back fizz a low ball towards the penalty spot where Aguero is waiting to lash home with a left-foot shot that gives the Southampton keeper no chance.

10 mins

GOAL KING

14 mins

#66

A Great Month

v Arsenal
14.12.2013

Sergio's prolific December continues with a stunning volley. Samir Nasri's corner is glanced towards the far post by defender Martin Demichelis and waiting to finish is Aguero, who spectacularly volleys home with the outside of his right boot.

AGÜERO

#67

Easy Does It
v Blackburn Rovers
15.01.2014

A fairly simple goal by Aguero's standards in a FA Cup third-round replay. Edin Dzeko plays a simple pass to his strike partner who pushes the ball to his left before firing a low shot into the net from close range.

73 mins

GOAL KING

79 mins

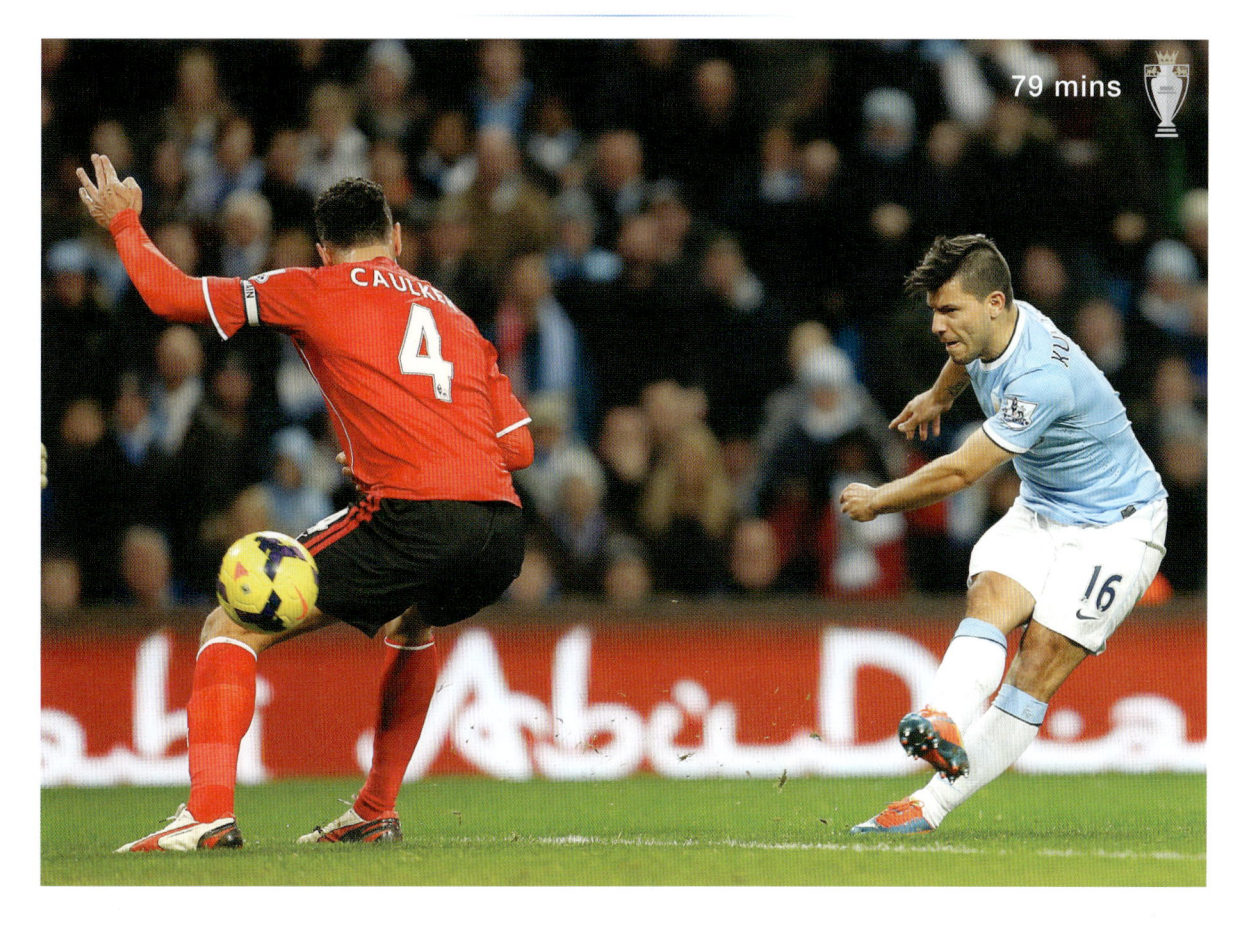

#68

A Constant Torment
v Cardiff City
18.01.2014

Collecting a short pass from Jesus Navas 30 yards out, Aguero carries the ball forward into the Cardiff box before jinking left, then right and thumping the ball home having tormented the Bluebirds' defender in the process.

AGÜERO

🏆 24 mins

GOAL KING

#69

Nothing To Worry About

v West Ham United 21.01.2014

With City already 6-0 up from the League Cup semi-final first leg, this was always going to be a comfortable night for the Blues at Upton Park and Sergio's goal is the result of yet more bad marking by Sam Allardyce's side. Marcos Lopes flicks the ball to Aguero who just about keeps possession before nudging it past a defender and tucking home with ease via a clever chip past the keeper.

AGÜERO

59 mins

#70

First Of Many
v Watford 25.01.2014

The first of a hat-trick against Watford, who led 2-0 in the FA Cup fourth round at the Etihad. Stevan Jovetic finds Aleks Kolarov on the left and his low cross is turned goalwards by Edin Dzeko but the keeper makes a fine save, only for Aguero to poke home the rebound from close range.

GOAL KING

78 mins

#71

Unstoppable

v Watford 25.01.2014

When Stevan Jovetic passes to Aguero midway through the Watford half, there seemed little threat, but Kun then moves forwards, cuts inside a defender and curls a beautiful shot with his left foot into the top corner from 18 yards out.

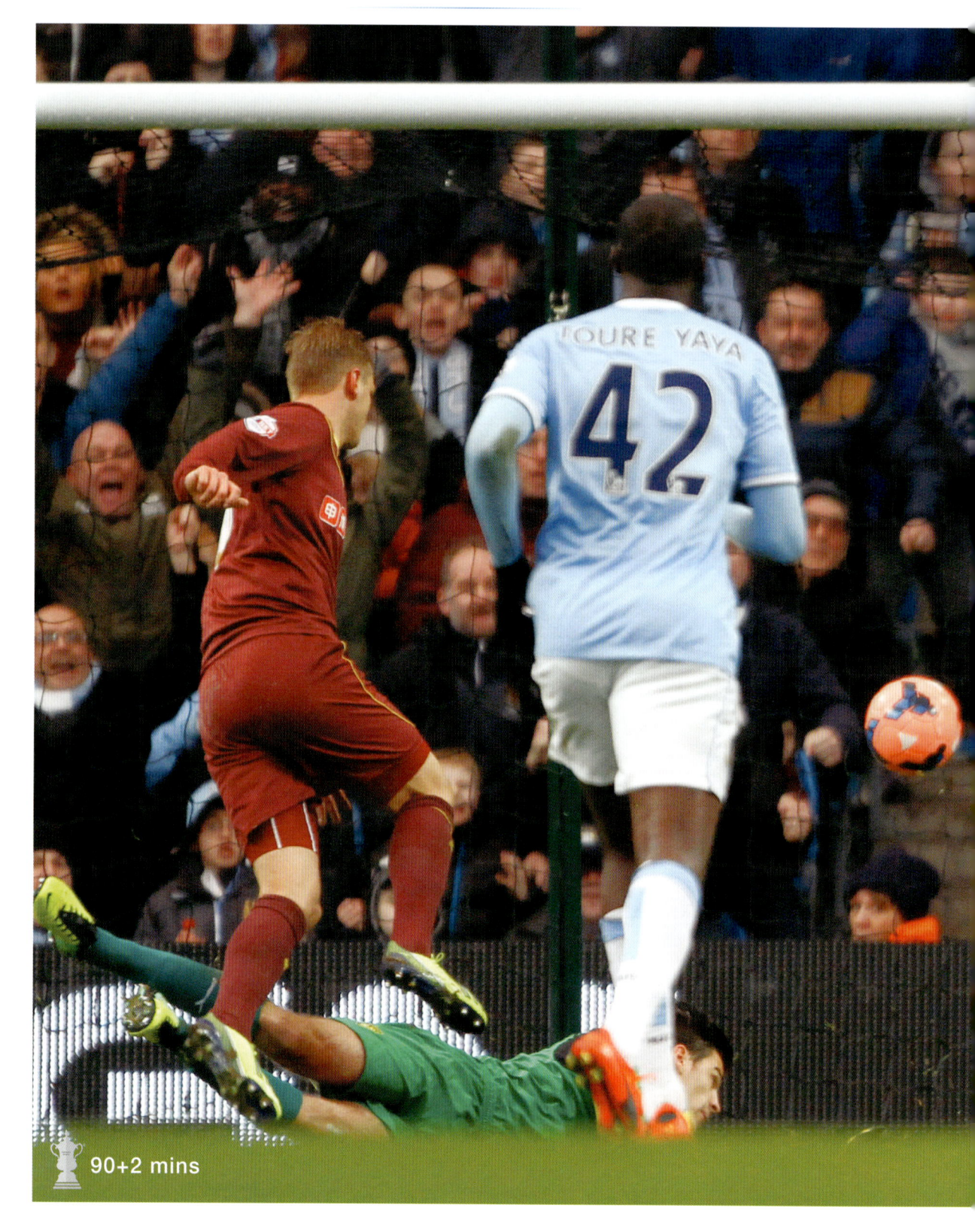

AGÜERO

90+2 mins

GOAL KING

#72

Triple Threat
v Watford
25.01.2014

Sergio completes his hat-trick against the Hornets with a header from Jesus Navas' looping cross to finally kill off a spirited Watford's FA Cup dreams.

15 mins

#73

Classy Finish

v Tottenham Hotspur
29.01.2014

Aguero's seventh goal in 14 days comes as David Silva spots his run into the Spurs box, plays a simple pass into his path and as Hugo Lloris comes out to the corner of the six-yard box Kun casually slips a delightful angled shot into the opposite corner. A classy finish from a striker at the top of his game.

AGÜERO

#74

Nice To Be Back
v West Bromwich Albion
21.04.2014

After a hamstring injury, this was Sergio's first goal for almost three months and what a way to return to scoring. He wriggles away from one challenge before lashing a shot from 25 yards out to put City 2-0 up on a day when fellow Argentines Pablo Zabaleta and Martin Demichelis also score.

10 mins

GOAL KING

22 mins

#75

Making It Count

v Everton

03.05.2014

A crucial goal and one that puts City back on course for a second Premier League title in three years. Aguero darts forward into the Everton box and fires a fierce low shot past Tim Howard to level the scores after the Blues had fallen behind on 11 minutes. It is Sergio's last act of the afternoon as he then limps off with a groin injury. But City go on to win 3-2 and climb to the top of the table with just two games remaining. It's his 28th goal of another stunning – though injury interrupted – season.

2014/15

SEASON

"It would be an honour to be able to reach 100 goals. But I'm not one to celebrate ahead of time. I do hope that if the goals come, they are securing us a win. Scoring is vital, sure, but if it isn't ensuring victory, a goal loses value"

42 GAMES
32 GOALS

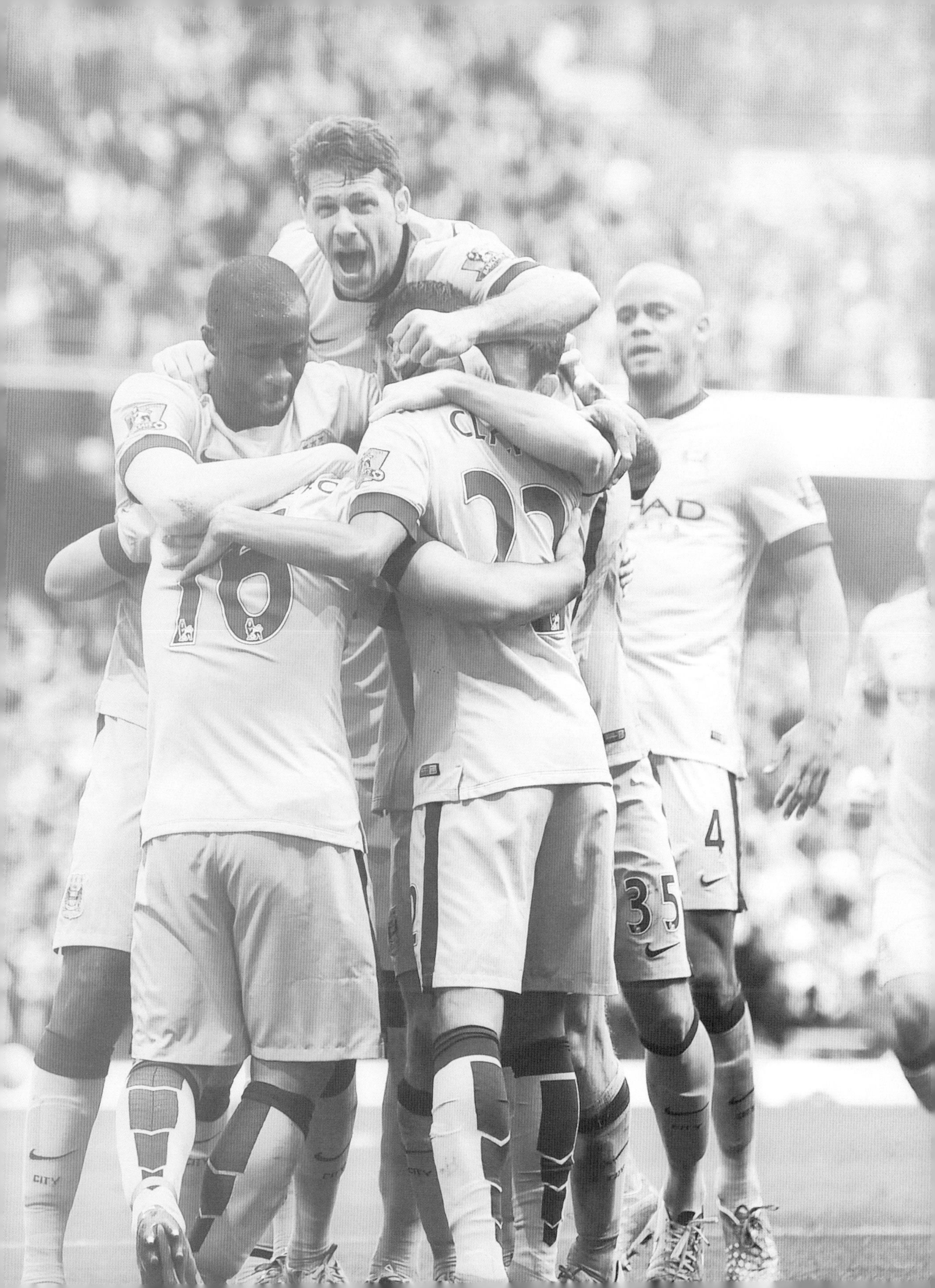
4
35

AGÜERO

#76

Two For Joy
v Newcastle United
17.08.2014

City are leading 1-0 at St James' Park but the hosts are still in the game until Aguero picks up the ball midway through the Newcastle half, heads into the box and past compatriot Fabricio Coloccini before firing a left-foot shot at Tim Krul. The Newcastle keeper saves the attempt but Sergio is first to the rebound and curls home right-footed from the corner of the six-yard box to seal a 2-0 win.

GOAL KING

90+2 mins

AGÜERO

69 mins

GOAL KING

#77

Straight Into Action
v Liverpool 25.08.2014

City are leading Liverpool by two goals when Sergio replaces Edin Dzeko on 68 minutes. Moments earlier, Jesus Navas had also come off the bench and the pair combine to devastating effect when Navas plays an inch-perfect pass in behind the Reds' defence from the right flank and into the path of Aguero. He tees himself up and then slips the ball past the keeper with only his second touch of the game.

AGÜERO

#78

Sergio's Satnav
v Arsenal
13.09.2014

Another goal created by Jesus Navas. The Spain winger manages to keep the ball in on the right flank before carrying play to the corner of the Arsenal box, picking out Aguero's clever run and delivering a low cross that the Argentine turns in from the edge of the six-yard box.

GOAL KING

28 mins

AGÜERO

7 mins

#79

Spinning And Winning
v Hull City 27.09.2014

Another fox-in-the-box goal. A corner from the left is swung across and Pablo Zabaleta's climbs highest on the edge of the box to head the ball down to Aguero, who spins on the edge of the six-yard box and rasps a shot into the corner of the net to give the keeper no chance.

GOAL KING

#80

Spot-kick Prowess
v Roma 30.09.2014

A further penalty to add to his collection, Aguero chases a cross into the box and is pulled back by former City defender Maicon. The referee spots the infringement and Aguero converts the penalty to give the Blues an early lead in the Champions League group stage clash at the Etihad.

4 mins

AGÜERO

#81

Leaving It Late
v Aston Villa
04.10.2014

City wait 82 minutes to break down Aston Villa's resistance with a Yaya Toure goal and Sergio then seals the points, shortly after. James Milner plays the ball to Aguero who controls the pass and nudges it to the right before rifling a powerful shot past Brad Guzan from the edge of the box.

88 mins

GOAL KING

13 mins

#82

What A Day
v Tottenham Hotspur
18.10.2014

The first of four against Spurs. Frank Lampard plays a simple pass to Aguero in the box and, after sizing up his options, he cuts back inside before hitting a low shot across the keeper and into the far corner to give the Blues an early lead.

AGÜERO

20 mins

#83

On A Roll

v Tottenham Hotspur 18.10.2014

Christian Eriksen had levelled for Spurs just two minutes after Kun's opening goal but City were soon back in front. James Milner plays a short pass into the path of Frank Lampard who is nudged in the back as he is about to collect the ball. The referee awards a spot-kick that Aguero comfortably dispatches for his second of the afternoon.

GOAL KING

#84

Spurs Brought To Heel
v Tottenham Hotspur
18.10.2014

Having missed a second penalty and then watched Spurs miss another, this crazy game saw the fourth penalty of the afternoon awarded on 66 minutes after Aguero was bundled over as he was about to turn home Jesus Navas' low cross. Aguero makes no mistake this time, completing his hat-trick and putting City 3-1 ahead.

66 mins

AGÜERO

#85

Four-some

v Tottenham Hotspur
18.10.2014

Sergio completes a memorable afternoon with a terrific solo effort as he dashes towards the right-hand side of the Spurs box chasing a Fernandinho pass before checking inside on to his left foot and hitting a low shot into the bottom left-hand corner of the net to complete a memorable game.

75 min

AGÜERO

29 mins

#86

From Russia With Love

v CSKA Moscow

21.10.2014

A vital Champions League goal in freezing Moscow comes when Edin Dzeko powers into the box yet with only the keeper to beat, he unselfishly passes to his right where Aguero has the simple task of planting the ball into the empty net.

GOAL KING

#87

Derby Winner
v Manchester United
02.11.2014

63 mins

In a tight Manchester derby, Kun Aguero once again makes all the difference. Yaya Toure plays a pass inside the United fullback for Gael Clichy to run on to – the Frenchman pulls the ball back into the area and finds Sergio on the edge of the six-yard box. The City striker then duly buries a left-foot shot powerfully past David De Gea from close range.

#88

World Class
v Queens Park Rangers
08.11.2014

32 mins

A classic goal from one of the world's best strikers. Sergio chases a long pass from Eliaquim Mangala before expertly bringing the ball down deftly, volleying it up gently before dropping his shoulder to the left and planting the ball past the keeper for a quite sublime goal.

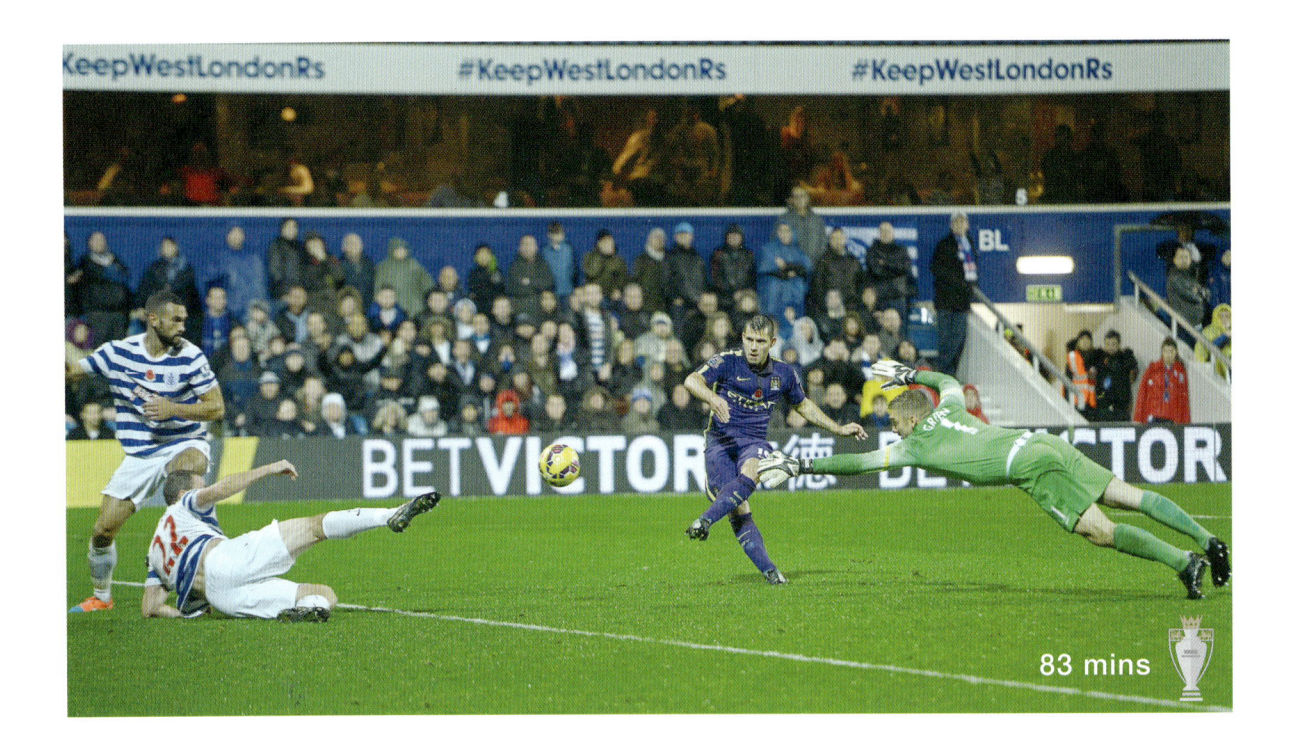

AGÜERO

83 mins

#89

A Strike From Nowhere
v Queens Park Rangers
08.11.2014

Another great goal out of nothing. Yaya Toure lofts a superb pass into the path of Sergio who chests the ball down, knocks it around the keeper before stopping the ball with his right foot and then planting the ball into the net with his left.

GOAL KING

#90

More Penalty Poise
v Bayern Munich
25.11.2014

Sergio is dragged down in the box as he is about to pull the trigger and the referee awards a penalty – Kun makes no mistake with a right-footed effort.

21 mins

AGÜERO

#91

Pouncing

v Bayern Munich 25.11.2014

A predatory strike from Sergio who, following an interception, latches on to the ball and drives forward before sending a low, left-foot shot past the keeper to make it 2-2.

85 mins

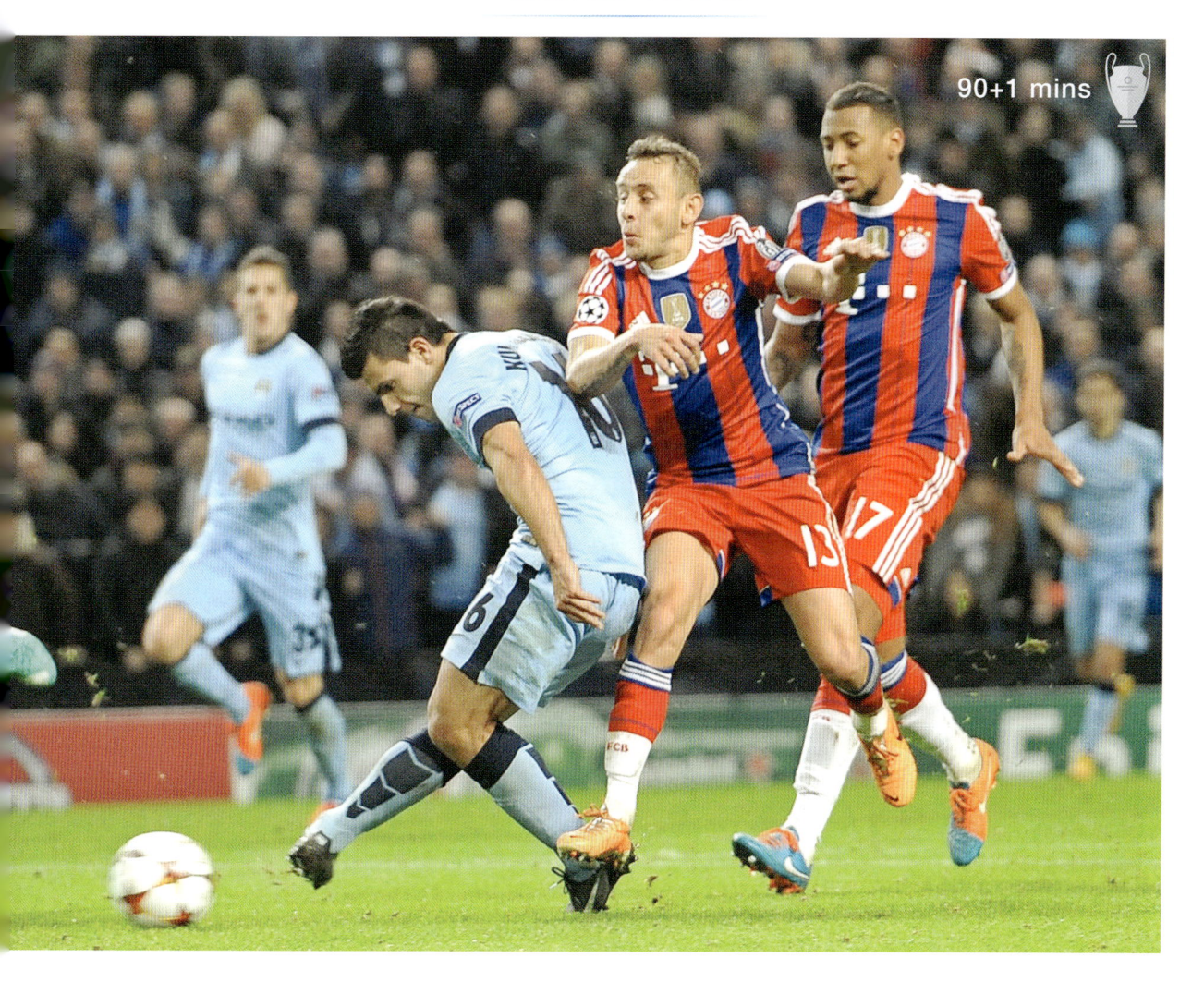

GOAL KING

90+1 mins

#92

Bayern Brilliance
v Bayern Munich 25.11.2014

A mistake from former City player Jerome Boateng enables Aguero to steal the ball and dash into the box. As three Bayern defenders close in, he places the ball past the keeper to complete his hat-trick and give City a dramatic 3-2 win over Pep Guardiola's side.

AGÜERO

21 mins

#93

Making The Difference

v Sunderland

03.12.2014

Having fallen behind to an early goal from Sunderland, Aguero rides one challenge outside the box before hitting a powerful shot past the home keeper from just inside the Sunderland penalty area.

GOAL KING

71 mins

#94

Beyond Doubt
v Sunderland 03.12.2014

City, now 3-1 up, put the result beyond doubt as James Milner's low cross is turned home by Sergio from seven yards out via the post for his second goal of the night and his 19th of an already prolific campaign.

#95

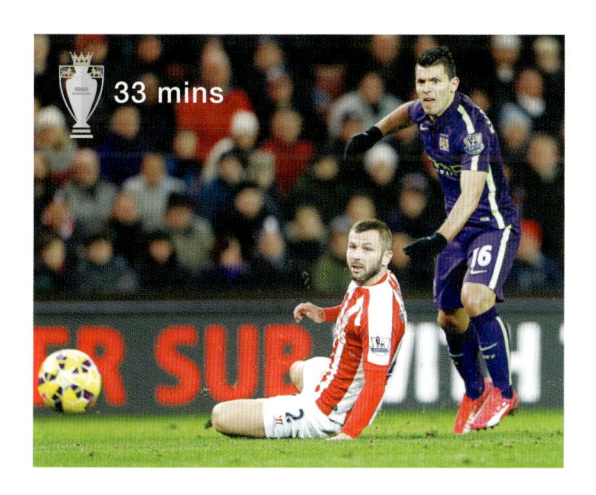

33 mins

Top Of The World
v Stoke City 11.02.2015

A battling goal and one made and scored by Sergio at his best. After winning a tussle just inside the Stoke half, Aguero bursts forward, weighs up his options before going inside the box and firing a low right-foot shot into the bottom left-hand corner of the net.

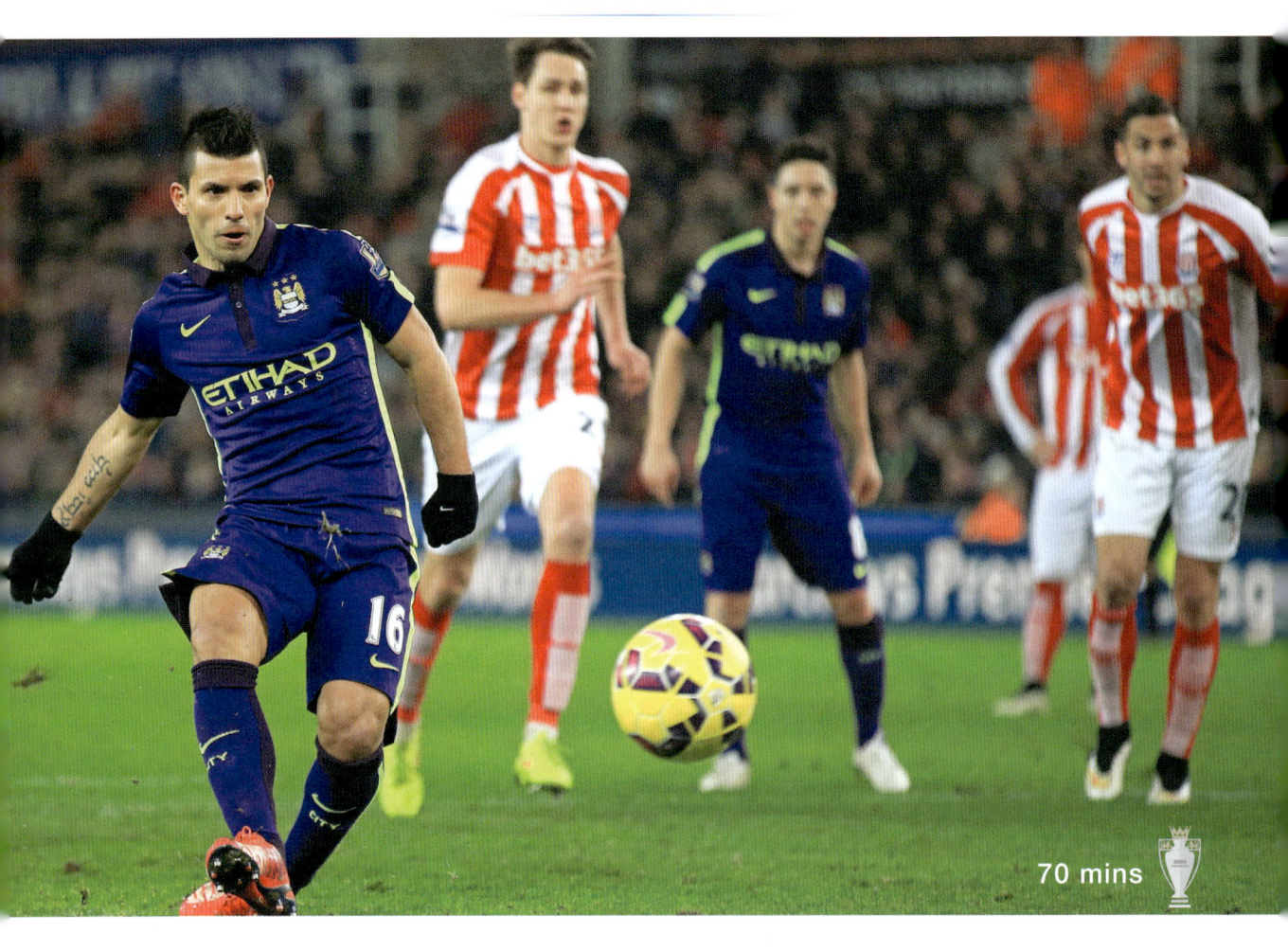

AGÜERO

70 mins

#96

Stoke Are Sunk

v Stoke City 11.02.2015

David Silva makes this goal after his dogged determination sees him spin from his marker in the box before being felled from behind as he moves clear. Aguero makes no mistake from the spot with a low shot into the bottom right-hand corner.

GOAL KING

#97

Penalties Aplenty
v Newcastle United
21.02.2015

Another penalty successfully dispatched by Aguero after Edin Dzeko had been fouled in the box in the opening minute of the match. It would be a long afternoon for Newcastle, who went on to lose 5-0.

2 mins

AGÜERO

69 mins

#98

Solo Sensation

v Barcelona

24.02.2015

A beauty. City are 2-0 behind to a Lionel Messi-inspired Barcelona side when Fernandinho plays a smart low ball to the edge of the box. David Silva's deft touch allows Sergio to take the ball on and fire a powerful shot past the keeper to halve the deficit.

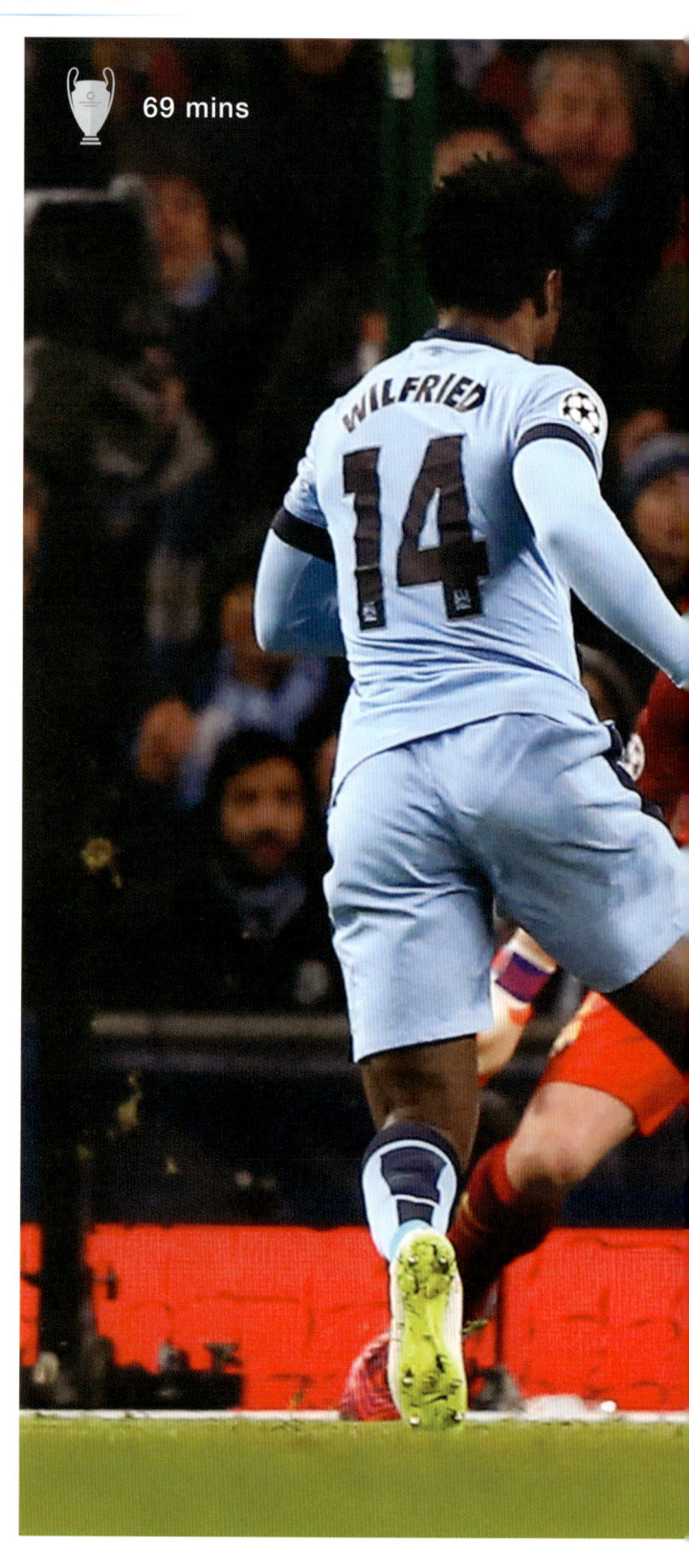

GOAL KING

AGÜERO

#99

Silva Lends A Hand

v Manchester United 12.04.2015

An early goal at Old Trafford. James Milner finds David Silva's run into the box and the Spaniard reaches the bye-line before firing a low cross into the six-yard box for Aguero to sweep home.

GOAL KING

#100

Raise Your Bat

v Manchester United
12.04.2015

Not the way Sergio would have wanted to celebrate his 100th Club goal. After leading 1-0, City find themselves 4-1 down and with just a minute or so remaining Frank Lampard spots Pablo Zabaleta's run into the box, finds him with a clever pass and Zaba's cross then finds Sergio on the edge of the six-yard box where he makes no mistake, despite David De Gea's best efforts.

89 mins

AGÜERO

36 mins

#101

Easily Done

v West Ham United 19.04.2015

Great work from Jesus Navas sees the pacey winger burst down the right into the West Ham penalty area and then deliver a neat cross into the middle for Aguero to sweep home with ease.

GOAL KING

#102

Breaking Brad
v Aston Villa 25.04.2015

A dreadful error by the Villa keeper. Brad Guzan receives a pass back and looks to knock it across the box to his full-back – but gets it horribly wrong and the advanced Kun Aguero collects the loose ball and rolls it into the empty net for one of his easiest goals yet for City.

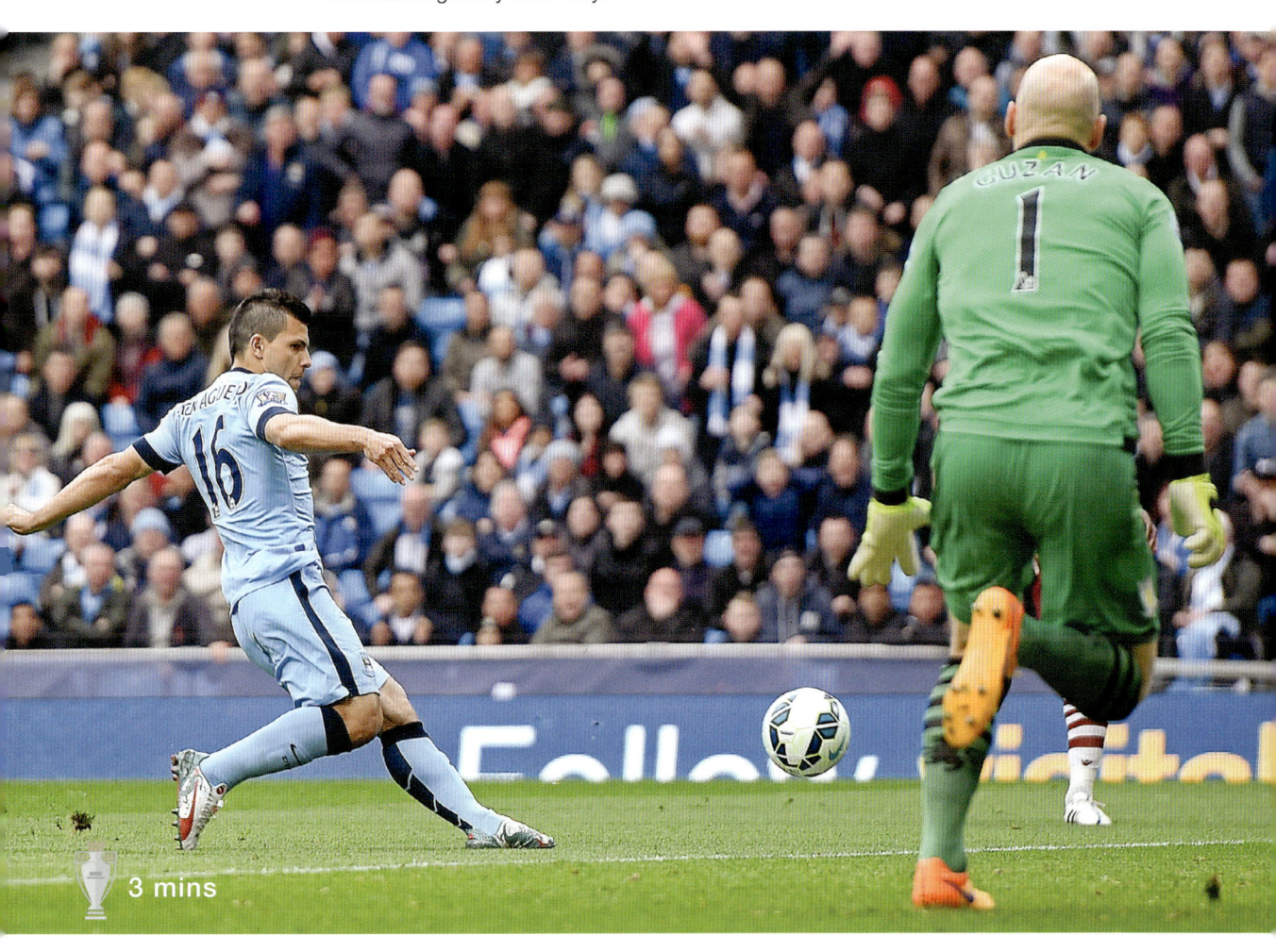

3 mins

AGÜERO

GOAL KING

29 mins

#103

Netting The Winner

v Tottenham Hotspur

03.05.2015

A beauty at White Hart Lane! A typical defence-splitting pass from David Silva as he spots Sergio's surge into the box and the Argentine looks up before hitting an angled shot over Hugo Lloris to score what proves to be the winning goal for the Blues.

AGÜERO

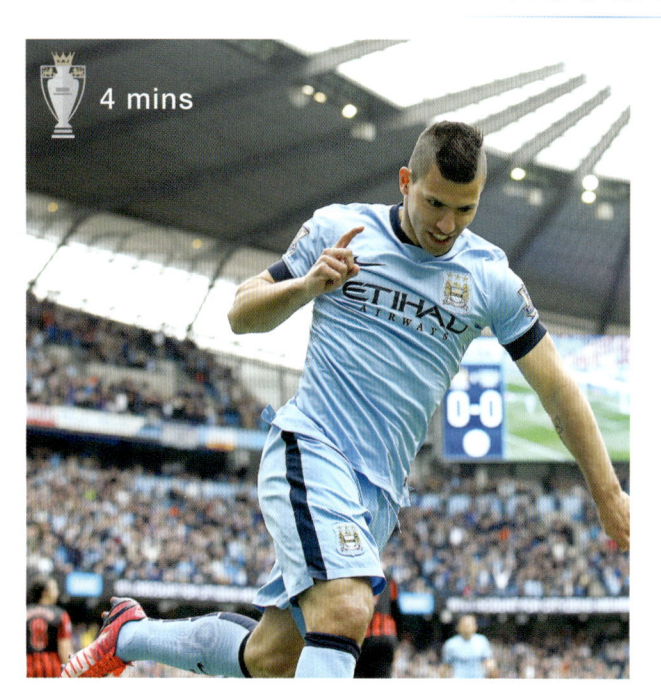

4 mins

#104

Early Lift

v QPR 10.05.2015

Not the prettiest of goals, this one is made and finished by Sergio who runs at the QPR defence and despite the presence of four defenders, he bundles through them all and sees the ball bounce kindly enough to lift it over the keeper and give City an early lead.

50 mins

#105

Doubling Up

v QPR
10.05.2015

Kun's second of the afternoon comes as a QPR defender attempts to control a clearance on the halfway line but instead gives the ball to Sergio, who sprints towards goal before coolly slotting the ball past the keeper from 10 yards.

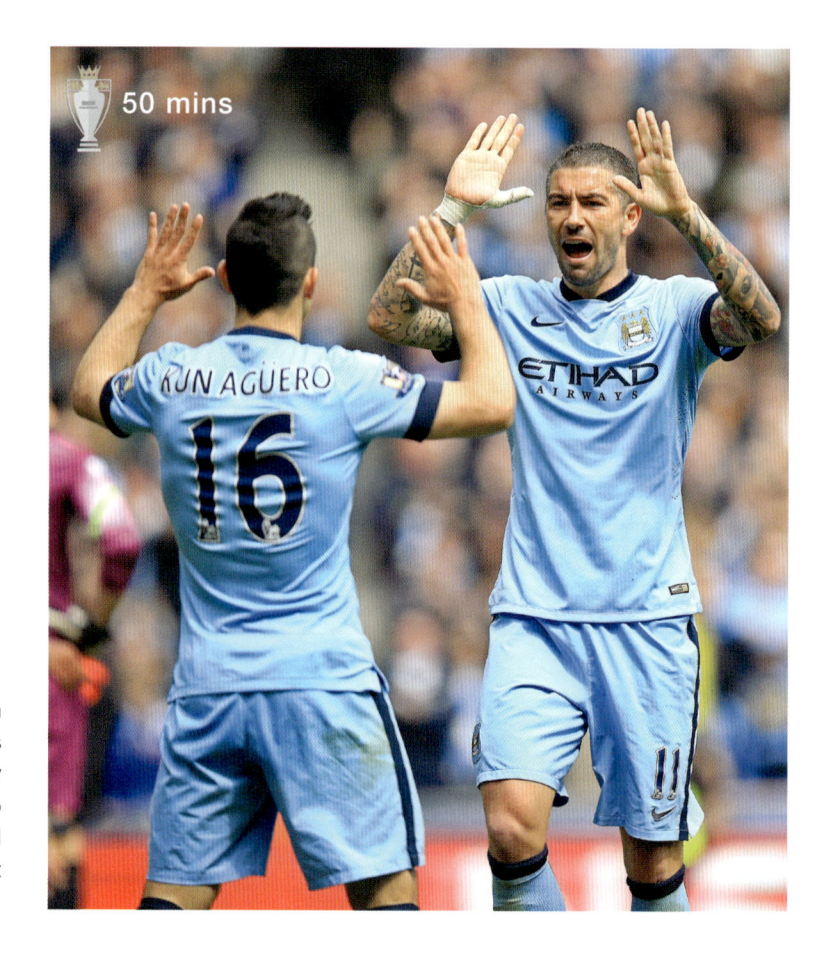

65 mins

#106

Fifth Time Lucky

v QPR
10.05.2015

Sergio completes his fifth hat-trick for City as he tucks away a penalty after David Silva had been fouled in the box.

AGÜERO

88 mins

GOAL KING

#107

Another Awesome Season
v Southampton 24.05.2015

Aguero ends the 2014/15 season with his 32nd goal in just 42 starts – an incredible return for a striker who finishes just one behind Golden Boot winner Harry Kane, who played more matches. It is another simple goal for Kun as Eliaquim Mangala heads the ball across the six-yard box where the unmarked Sergio nods into an empty net to complete another stunning season's work.

2015/16
SEASON

Manchester City

"I am well aware of the affection that City's supporters have shown towards me. I have felt it since day one, on and off the pitch. This is a great incentive for me to attempt to pay them back, day by day"

44 GAMES
29 GOALS

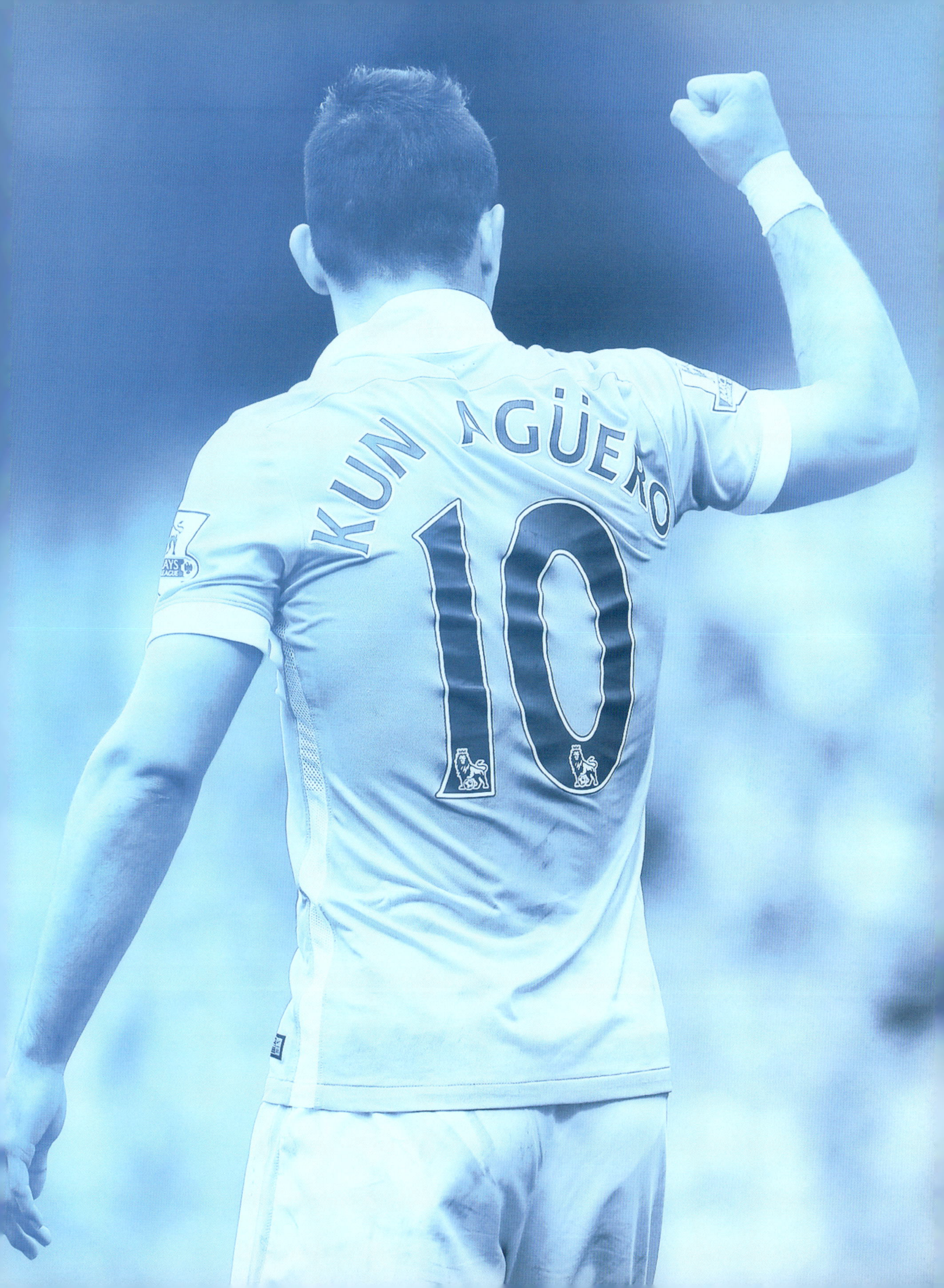
KUN AGÜERO
10

AGÜERO

#108

Amazing Start
v Chelsea 16.08.2015

What a start to the new campaign for City and Kun as the Blues thrash Chelsea 3-0 at the Etihad. Yaya Toure plays a simple pass into Aguero who chests the ball down, shows fantastic close control to edge it away from a defender to open up a yard of space and then calmly rolls a shot past Asmir Begovic to put City ahead.

31 mins

GOAL KING

9 mins

#109

Cup Fun
v Sunderland 22.09.2015

Sergio thumps home another penalty after Jesus Navas had been fouled in the box to put the Blues on the way to a 4-1 League Cup win at the Stadium of Light.

#110

Repeat Effort

v Borussia Mönchengladbach
30.09.2015

Yet another successful penalty! Sergio is fouled in the box and converts the spot-kick himself with a low shot into the bottom right-hand corner to give City a last-gasp 2-1 win away to Borussia Mönchengladbach.

90 mins

GOAL KING

42 mins

#111

Just The Start

v Newcastle United

03.10.2015

City trail 1-0 to Newcastle until David Silva's clever chip finds Fernandinho, who heads across the six-yard box and Aguero nods home the equaliser from close range. It's the first goal of an incredible afternoon for Kun.

AGÜERO

49 mins

#112

Cruel For Krul

v Newcastle United 03.10.2015

Feeding off a pass from David Silva, Aguero works himself a yard of space on the edge of the box before firing a left-foot shot that deflects past Tim Krul to put City ahead. Untidy, but they all count!

GOAL KING

#113

Three In Eight
v Newcastle United
03.10.2015

Great vision from Kevin De Bruyne releases Aguero who runs in behind the Newcastle defence, waits for the goalkeeper to come towards him before he then gently lifts the ball over Krul and into the far corner of the net – a third goal in eight minutes and City's quickest hat-trick ever. But Kun's day was far from over…

50 mins

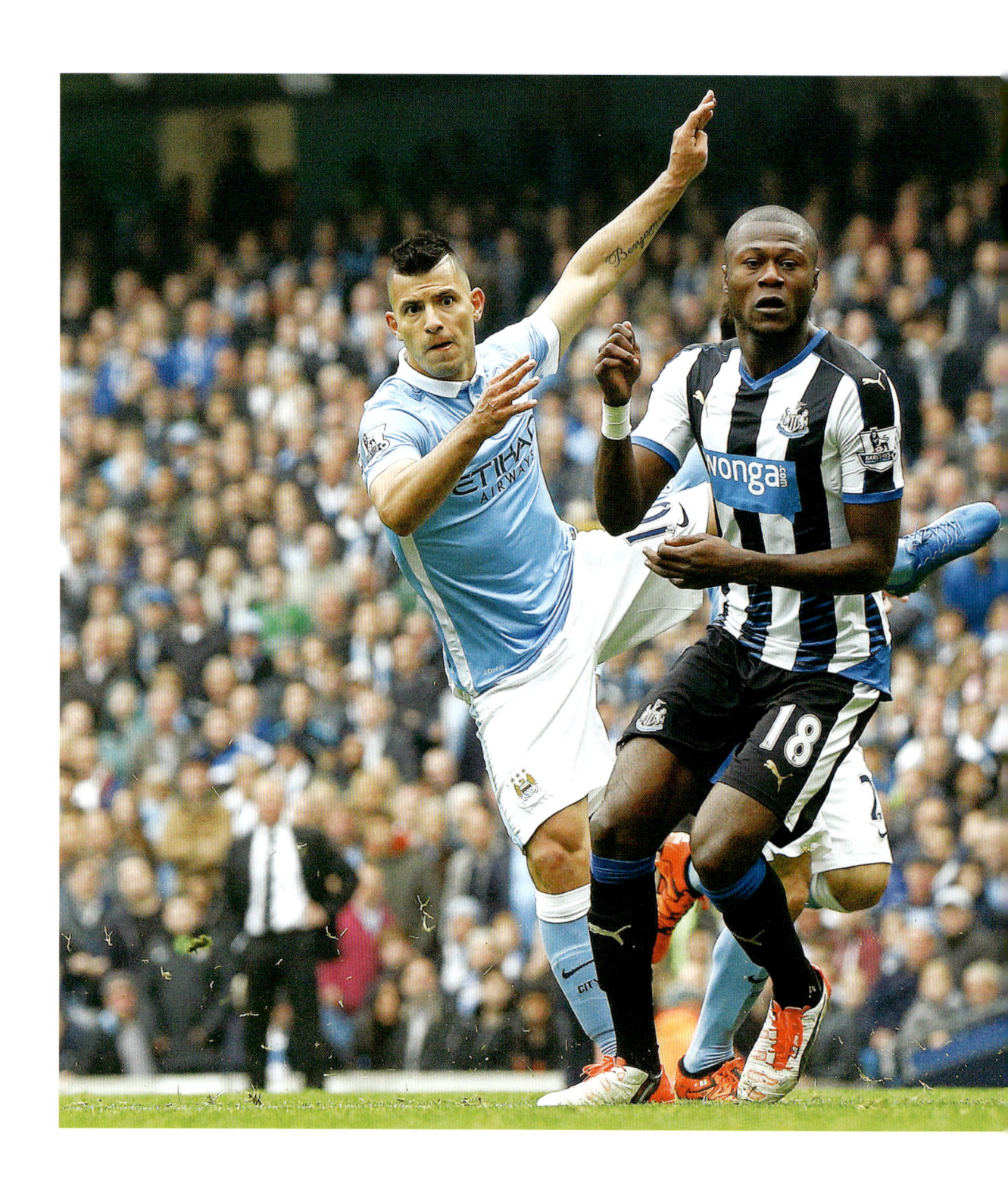

AGÜERO

GOAL KING

60 mins

#114

More Still To Come
v Newcastle United
03.10.2015

Sergio's fourth this afternoon. David Silva again spots Kun in space, this time on the left, and he cuts inside one challenge before firing a right-foot shot low and hard past Krul and into the bottom right-hand corner of the net. A superb finish from a striker at the very top of his game and the second time he'd hit four goals in one match for the Blues – but he still wasn't finished…

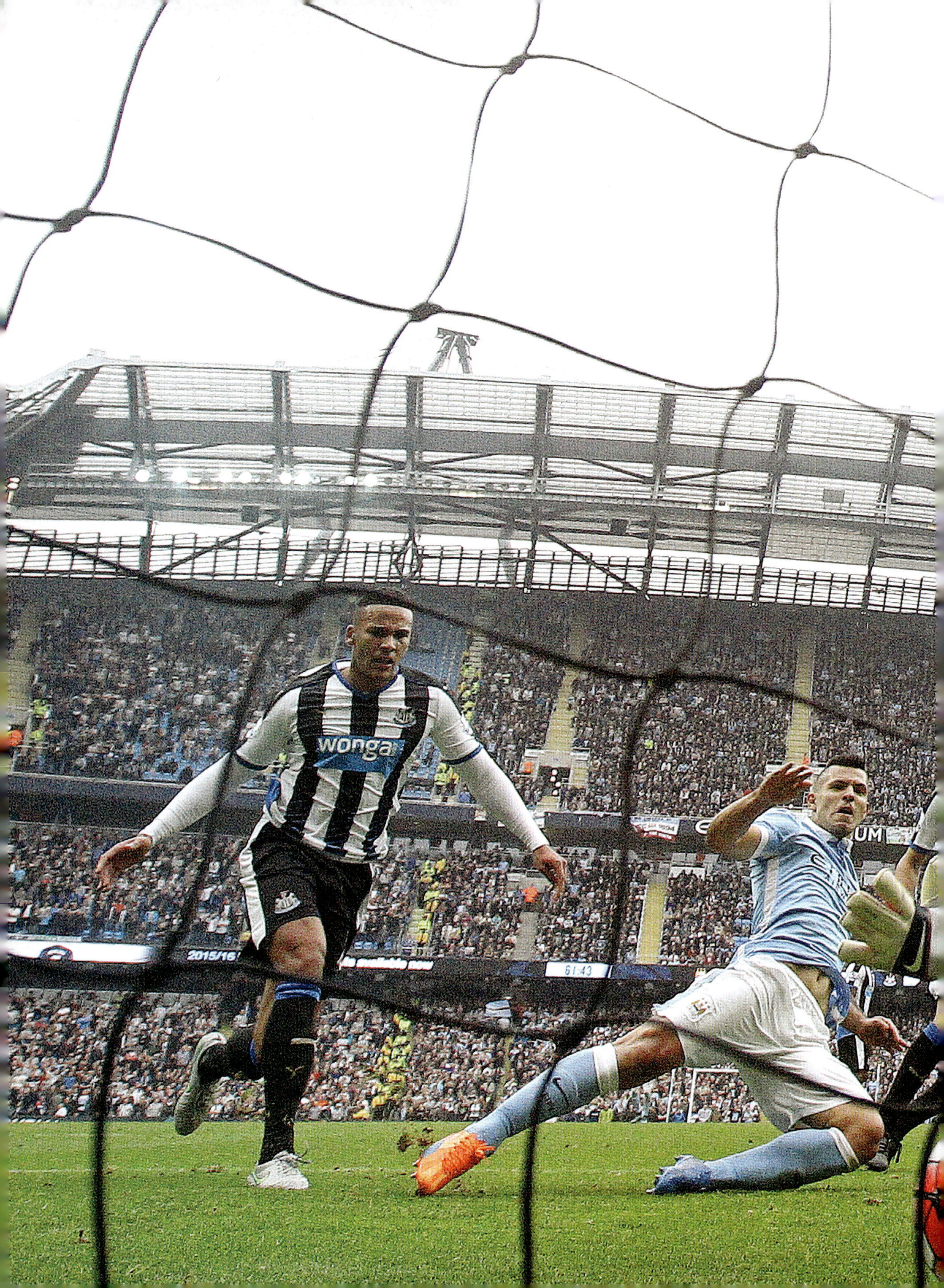
wonga
2015/16
61:43

#115

Simply Incredible
v Newcastle United
03.10.2015

A fifth goal in just 20 minutes' playing time, this was all about the vision of Kevin De Bruyne and the predatory instincts of Kun Aguero. De Bruyne receives the ball but is facing away from goal when he pivots around to cross low into the six-yard box for Sergio to slide home from close range. An amazing spell of finishing by the Argentine.

62 mins

AGÜERO

#116

Fighting Back
v Liverpool 21.11.2015

City have been systematically taken apart by Jurgen Klopp's Liverpool and are 3-0 down with barely 30 minutes played. Taking the bull by the horns, Aguero picks the ball up and heads towards goal. With just a minute of the opening period remaining, he cuts in slightly from the left, bamboozles Lucas Leiva, and hits a fierce right-foot shot past Simon Mignolet from fully 20 yards out.

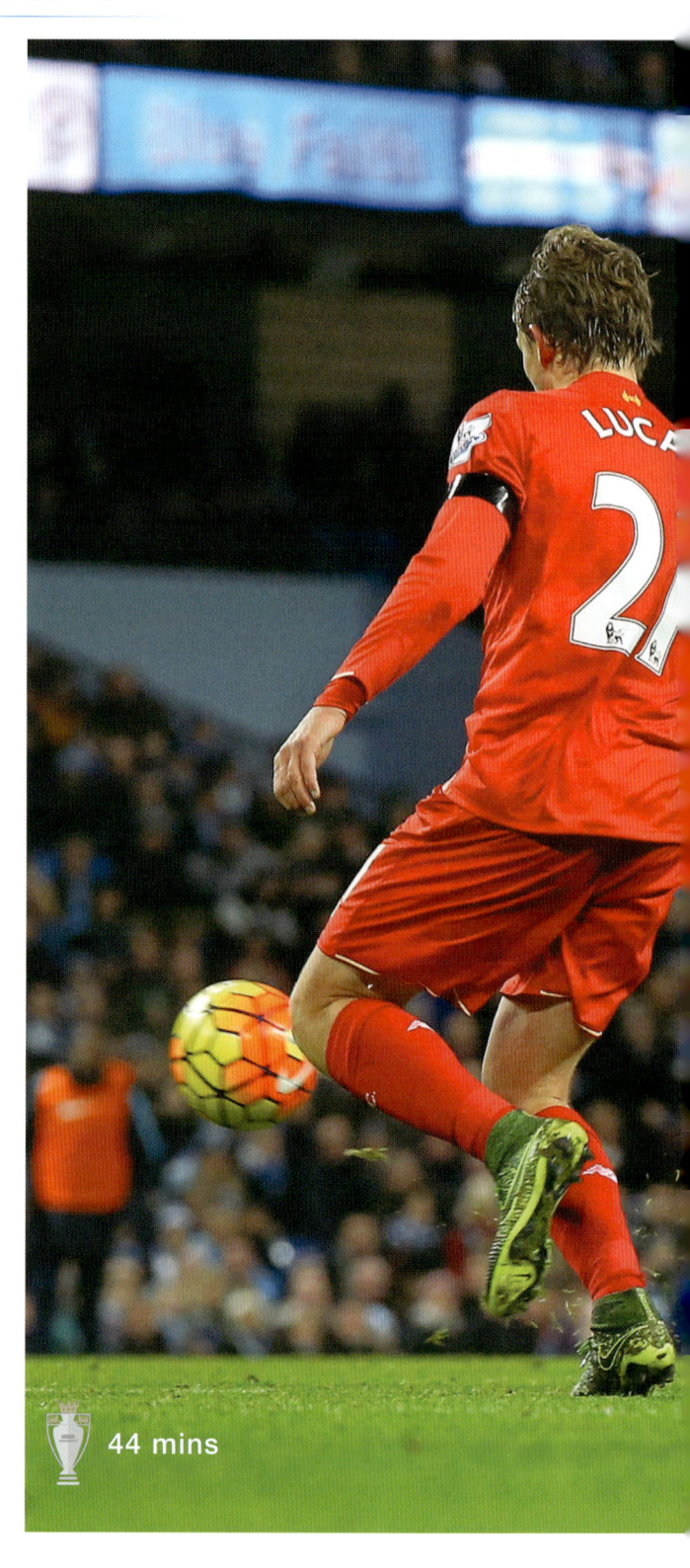

44 mins

GOAL KING

AGÜERO

#117

Drama Aplenty
v Watford
02.01.2016

City trailed 1-0 to the Hornets but managed to get on level terms shortly before Aguero's goal. Bacary Sagna's deep cross into the box finds the head of Sergio, who almost hangs in the air before nodding a well-placed header just out of the reach of Heurelho Gomes for a dramatic late winner.

84 mins

#118

One Of His Best
v Norwich City
09.01.2016

16 mins

Simply stunning. Aguero collects a back-heeled pass 30 yards from goal, he jinks past two defenders in the blink of an eye, sells another a dummy as he enters the box and then plants the ball past the goalkeeper – all within the space of six blistering seconds!

GOAL KING

#119

They All Count

v Crystal Palace
16.01.2016

Slightly fortuitous by Kun's standards, he hits a shot from 25 yards that deflects off Palace defender Scott Dann's head and past the keeper for City's second goal of the afternoon.

41 mins

68 mins

#120

Poise Against Palace

v Crystal Palace
16.01.2016

If his first of the afternoon had been a little fortunate, his second is anything but as a sweeping City move tears the Palace defence to shreds and ends as Kevin De Bruyne plays a simple pass to Sergio, who only has to tap home from six yards out.

#121

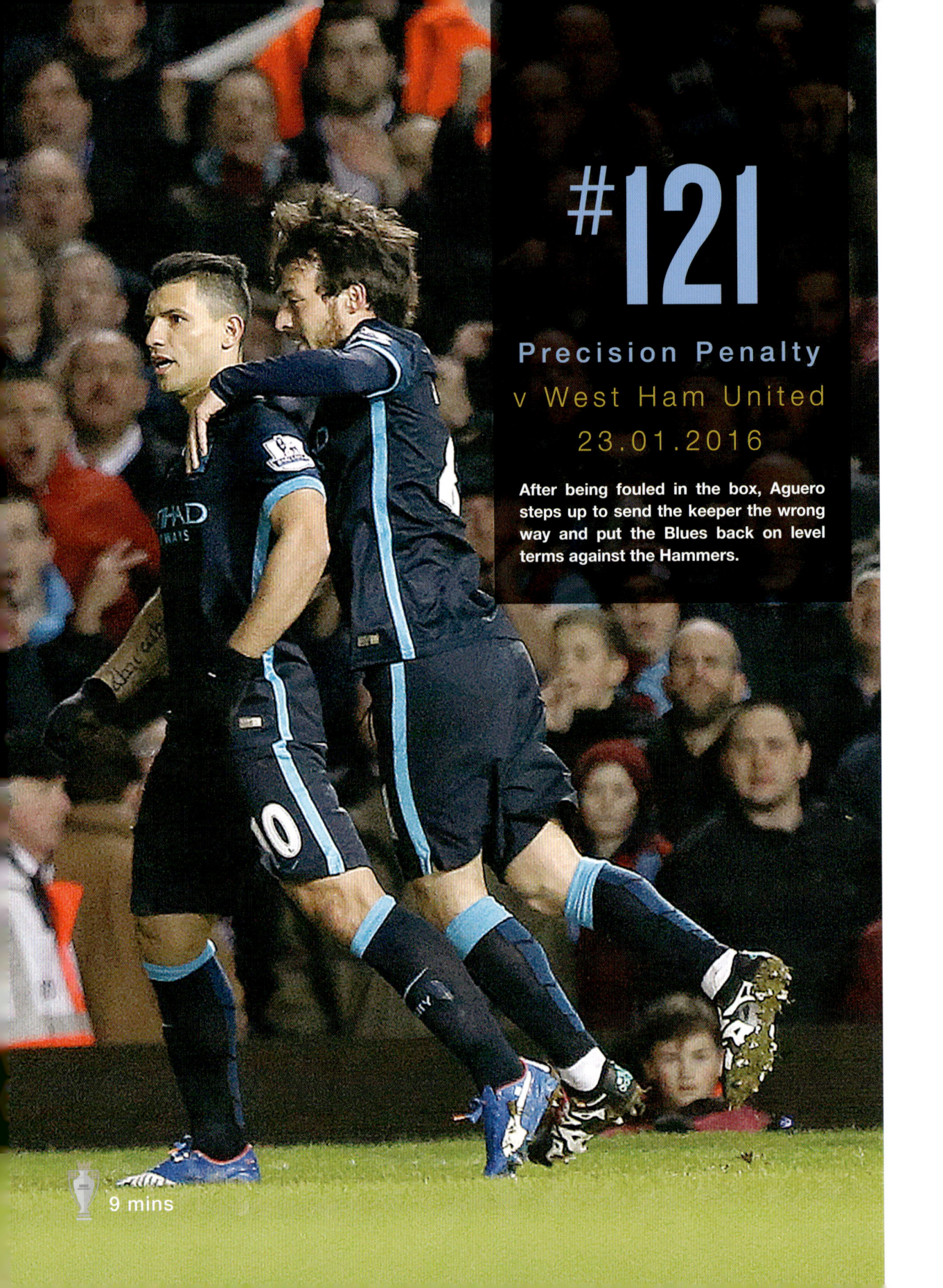

Precision Penalty

v West Ham United
23.01.2016

After being fouled in the box, Aguero steps up to send the keeper the wrong way and put the Blues back on level terms against the Hammers.

9 mins

GOAL KING

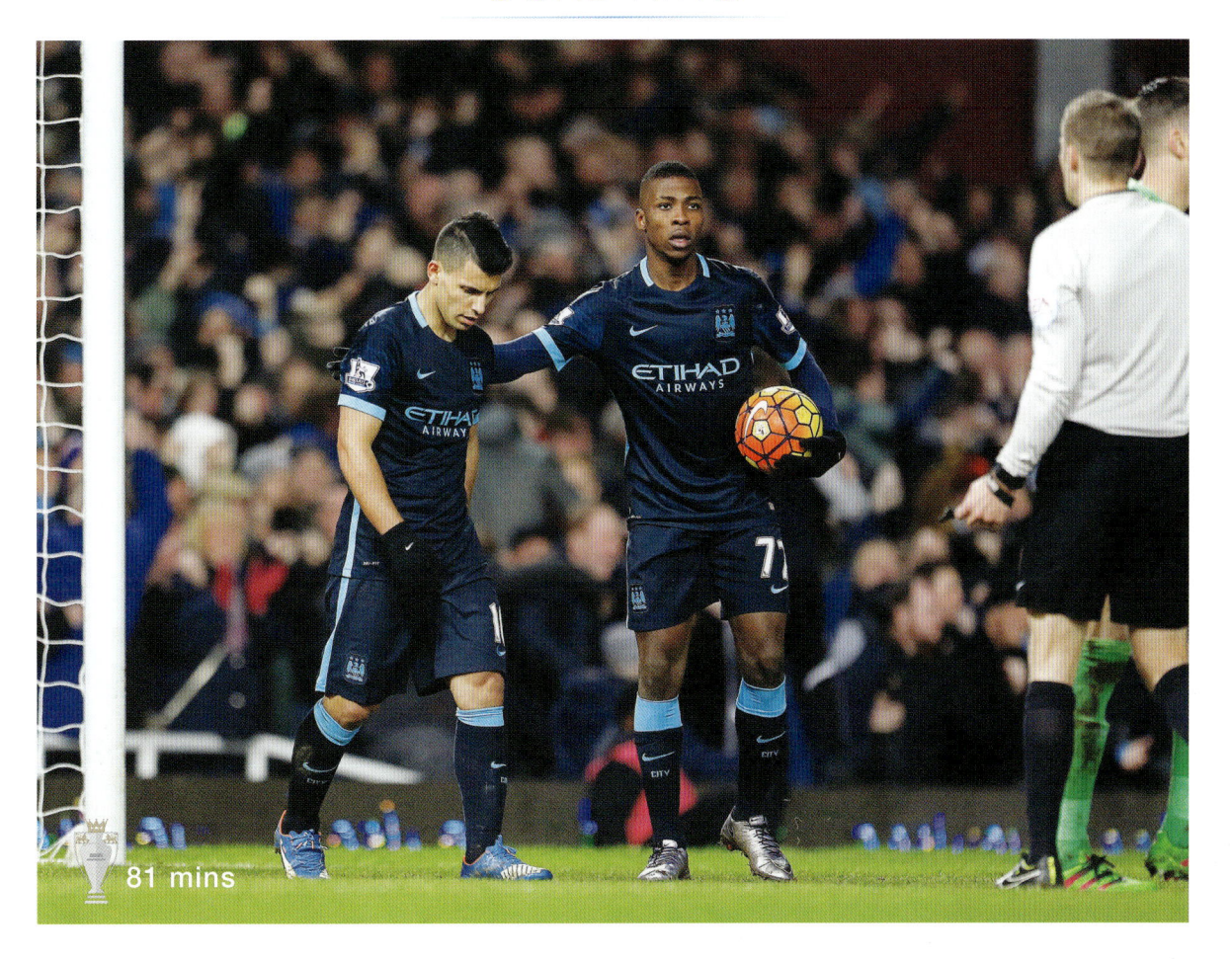

81 mins

#122

Hurting The Hammers
v West Ham United
23.01.2016

Kelechi Iheanacho is tackled on the edge of the West Ham box but the ball only falls into the path of Aguero, who makes no mistake from seven yards out with a confident finish.

AGÜERO

78 mins

#123

So Clever
v Everton 27.01.2016

A stunning goal that sends City to Wembley, Kevin De Bruyne whips in a superb cross towards the penalty spot and Sergio cleverly guides a powerful header past the keeper by allowing the pace of the ball to do the hard work – a fantastic goal that sends the Etihad wild.

GOAL KING

#124

High And Dry
v Sunderland
02.02.2016

16 mins

A low cross by Jesus Navas finds Aguero eight yards from goal and after moving past the defender with his left foot, he then pokes it high over the keeper and into the corner of the net with his right.

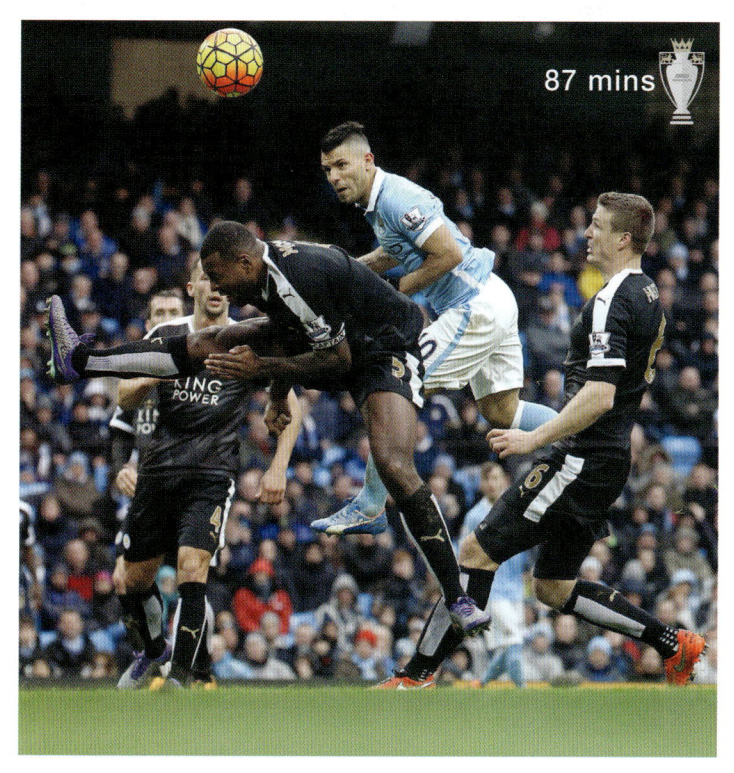

87 mins

#125

Outfoxed
v Leicester City
06.02.2016

A cracking header worthy of winning any game, but sadly this top-of-the-table clash with Leicester City was already decided by the time Aguero rose to meet Bersant Celina's fine cross, heading powerfully past Kasper Schmeichel from a difficult angle to make the score 1-3 in the Foxes' favour.

AGÜERO

15 mins

#126

Dynamic

v Dynamo Kyiv

24.02.2016

A static Kyiv defence is punished as City take an early lead in the first leg of the Champions League Round of 16 tie in Ukraine. Yaya Toure heads down a cross to Aguero who has time to tee up a shot before firing past the home keeper, setting the Blues on their way to a priceless 3-1 victory.

GOAL KING

#127

Lucky Break
v Aston Villa
05.03.2016

Former City defender Micah Richards is a shade unfortunate as he attempts to clear a ball into the Villa box, only to see his tackle cannon off the shins of ex-teammate Aguero and into the net.

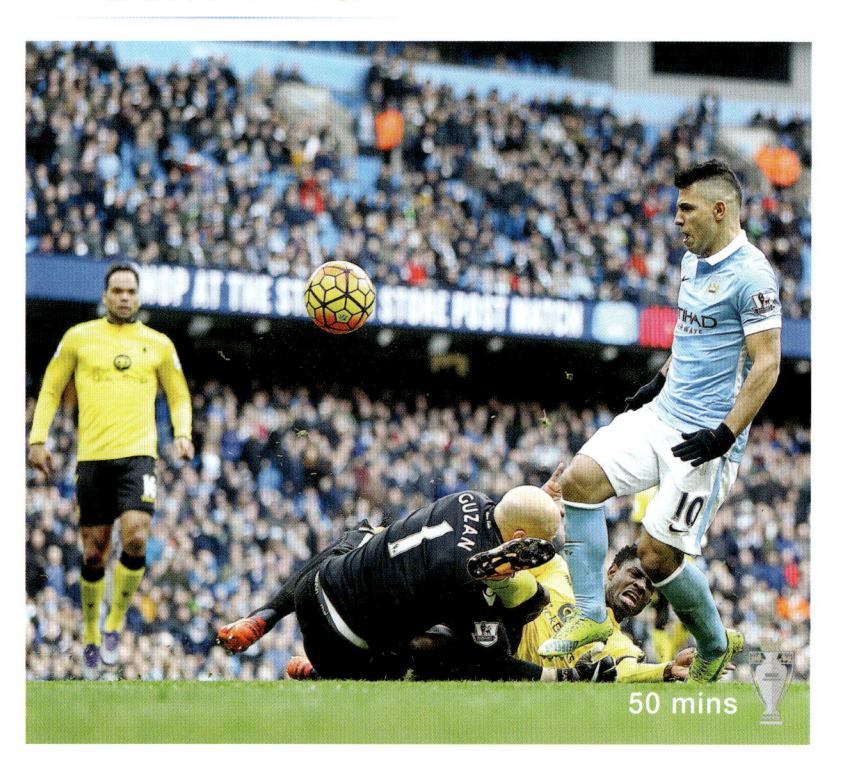

50 mins

60 mins

#128

What A Combo
v Aston Villa
05.03.2016

There is no luck about this wonderfully worked goal that begins with Sergio outside the box. He dinks the ball to David Silva who lofts a return pass over the defenders and into Kun's path. Aguero chests it down and then squeezes a shot past the keeper on his near post as City make it three goals in the space of 12 second-half minutes.

AGÜERO

19 mins

#129

Kun On Rampage
v Bournemouth
02.04.2016

A rampant City go three goals up within the first 20 minutes at the Vitality Stadium. Jesus Navas whips a high cross into the six-yard box that Aguero leaps for, and his header creeps over the line despite the defender's desperate attempt at a clearance.

GOAL KING

#130

History Boy
v West Bromwich Albion
09.04.2016

Though a penalty, this is a landmark goal for Kun, who enters the Blues' all-time top 10 goal-scorers list with his 130th strike for the Club, as well as celebrating his 200th appearance. The penalty is awarded for a foul on Aleks Kolarov and comfortably dispatched by Sergio.

19 mins

AGÜERO

#131

Powerful Precision
v Chelsea
16.04.2016

The start of a memorable afternoon for Sergio. Some 20 yards out, he pushes the ball to his right and past a defender before hitting a low shot into the bottom right-hand corner with unnerving accuracy and power.

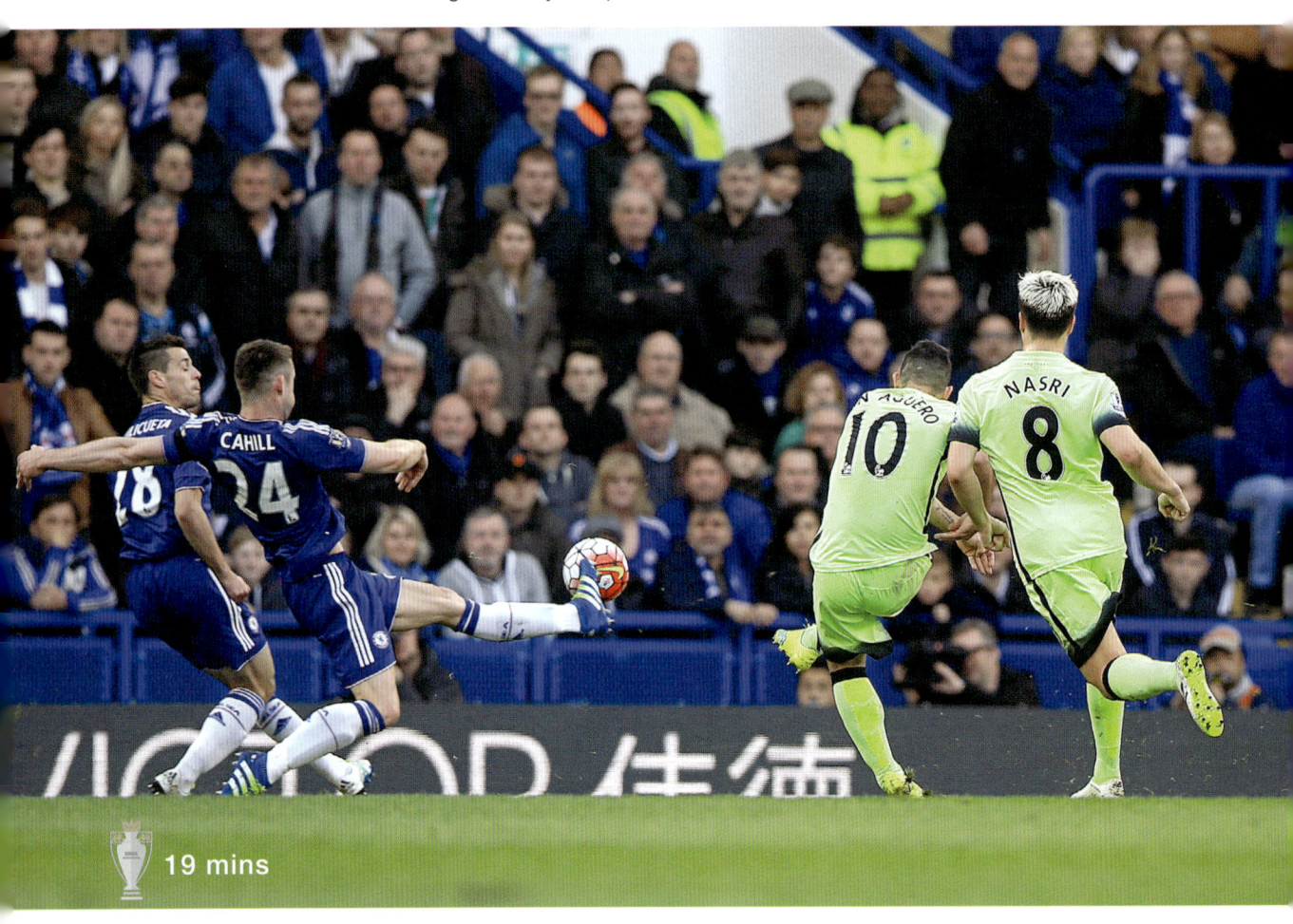

19 mins

GOAL KING

54 mins

#132

Ruthless Brilliance
v Chelsea
16.04.2016

Holding his run until the perfect moment, Aguero latches on to a superbly weighted through ball from Samir Nasri before lashing a rising shot over keeper Thibaut Courtois from eight yards out. Clinical.

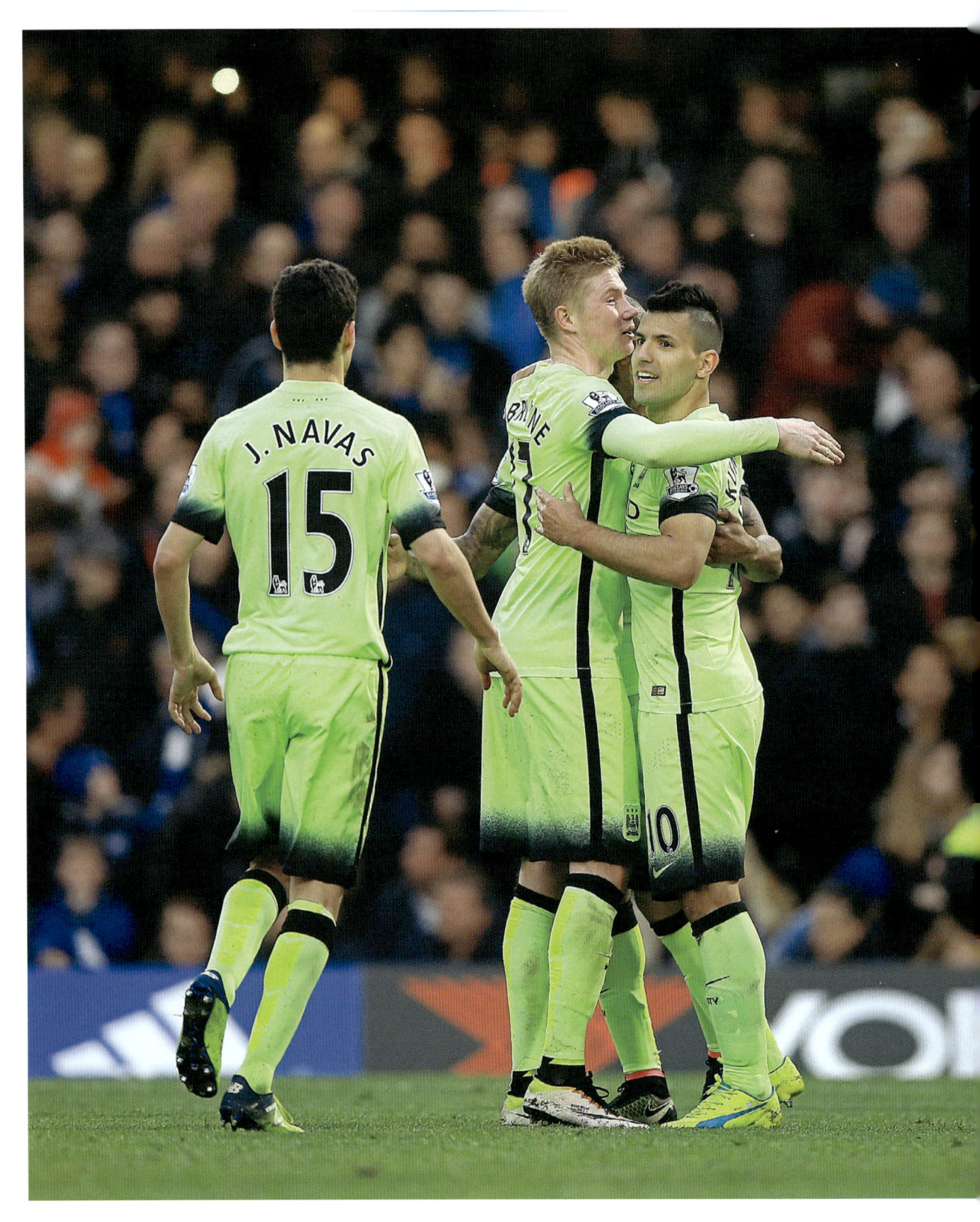

AGÜERO

GOAL KING

80 mins

#133

Getting Better And Better
v Chelsea
16.04.2016

When Fernandinho is fouled by keeper Thibaut Courtois, the home keeper is shown a straight red card, and sub Asmir Begovic's first job is to collect the ball out of the net after Aguero sends him the wrong way to complete his hat-trick – perhaps his most impressive yet.

AGÜERO

14 mins

#134

Unbelievable
v Newcastle United
19.04.2016

This goal was all about the delivery, with Aleks Kolarov providing a precise, whipped in cross for Aguero to leap and guide into the net for a superb headed goal against the Magpies.

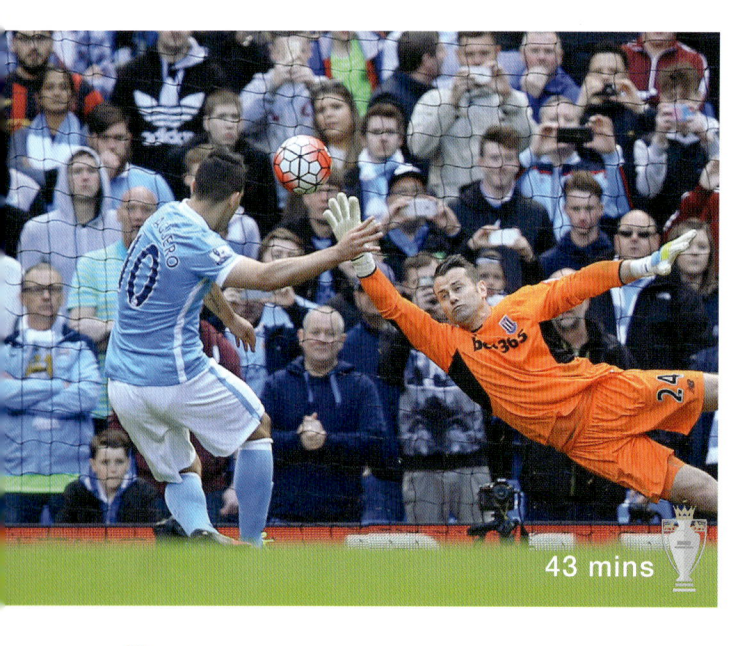

#135

Given No Chance
v Stoke City
23.04.2016

Goal No.28 of another prolific campaign, Kun Aguero makes no mistake from the penalty spot to put the Blues 2-0 up against the Potters after Kelechi Iheanacho is brought down by Ryan Shawcross in the penalty area.

43 mins

GOAL KING

8 mins

#136

Left-Foot Magic

v Arsenal 08.05.2016

Fernandinho's cushioned header finds Sergio on the edge of the Arsenal box and he spins away from his marker before firing a powerful left-foot shot in from just inside the 18-yard line.

2016/17
SEASON

"It's true that when a season starts, it's easy to believe you're only going upwards. However, at this particular moment, with Pep's arrival, I feel like this might be one of the best ones yet"

45 GAMES
33 GOALS

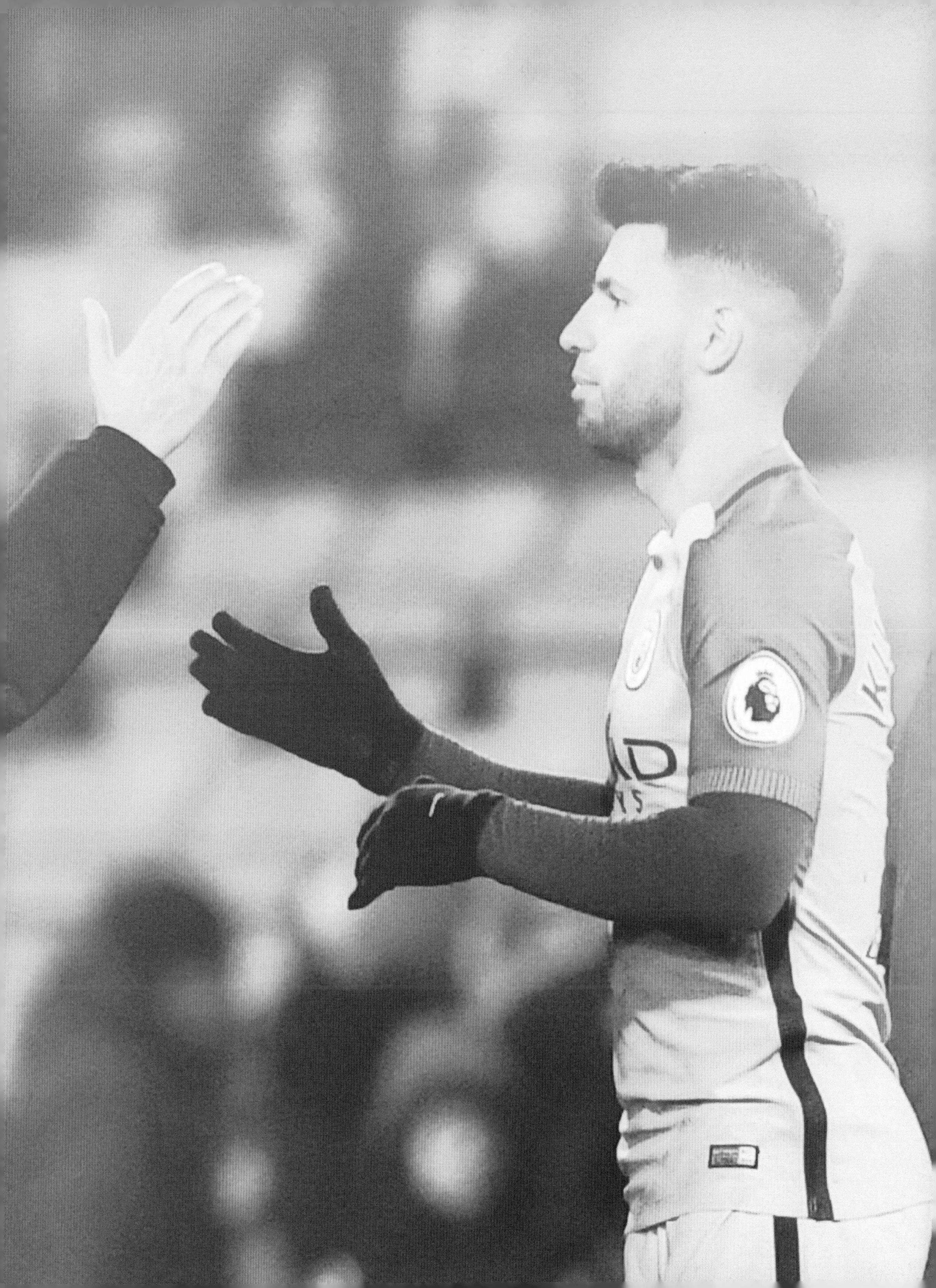

4 mins

#137

Plenty of Pep
v Sunderland
13.08.2016

When Raheem Sterling is fouled in the box, there's only one man who is going to step up and finish the job off and that man, of course, is Sergio Aguero, who plants a powerful penalty kick high to the keeper's left to put City 1-0 up just four minutes into Pep Guardiola's Premier League reign.

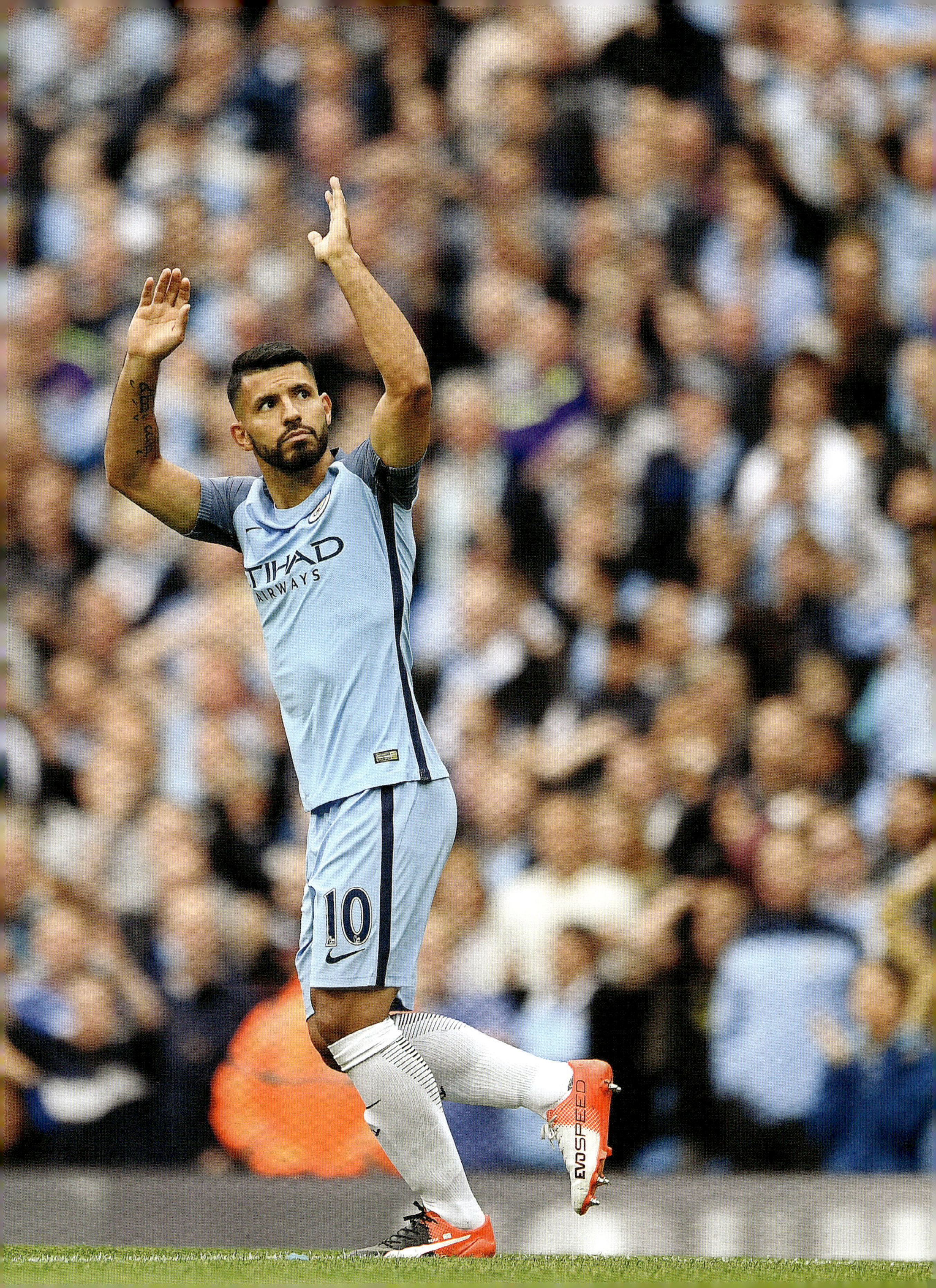
TIHAD
AIRWAYS
10
EVOSPEED

AGÜERO

41 mins

GOAL KING

#138
Two More To Follow
v Steaua Bucharest
16.08.2016

The first goal of yet another hat-trick for the irrepressible Argentina star. This time a ball on the edge of the Steaua box is controlled by Raheem Sterling and Aguero does the rest, placing a shot past the home keeper in this Champions League play-off first leg.

#139
Europe's Finest
v Steaua Bucharest
16.08.2016

Neat work by Nolito, Kevin De Bruyne and Aguero puts this tie out of Steaua's reach as Nolito eventually plays a short pass to his right in the box for Kun to fire past the keeper.

78 mins

89 mins

#140

Powering Forward

v Steaua Bucharest
16.08.2016

Sergio completes Steaua's misery by collecting the ball some 40 yards from goal, powering forward to the edge of the box before unleashing a shot that hits the post and spins into the opposite corner to complete another hat-trick for the Blues.

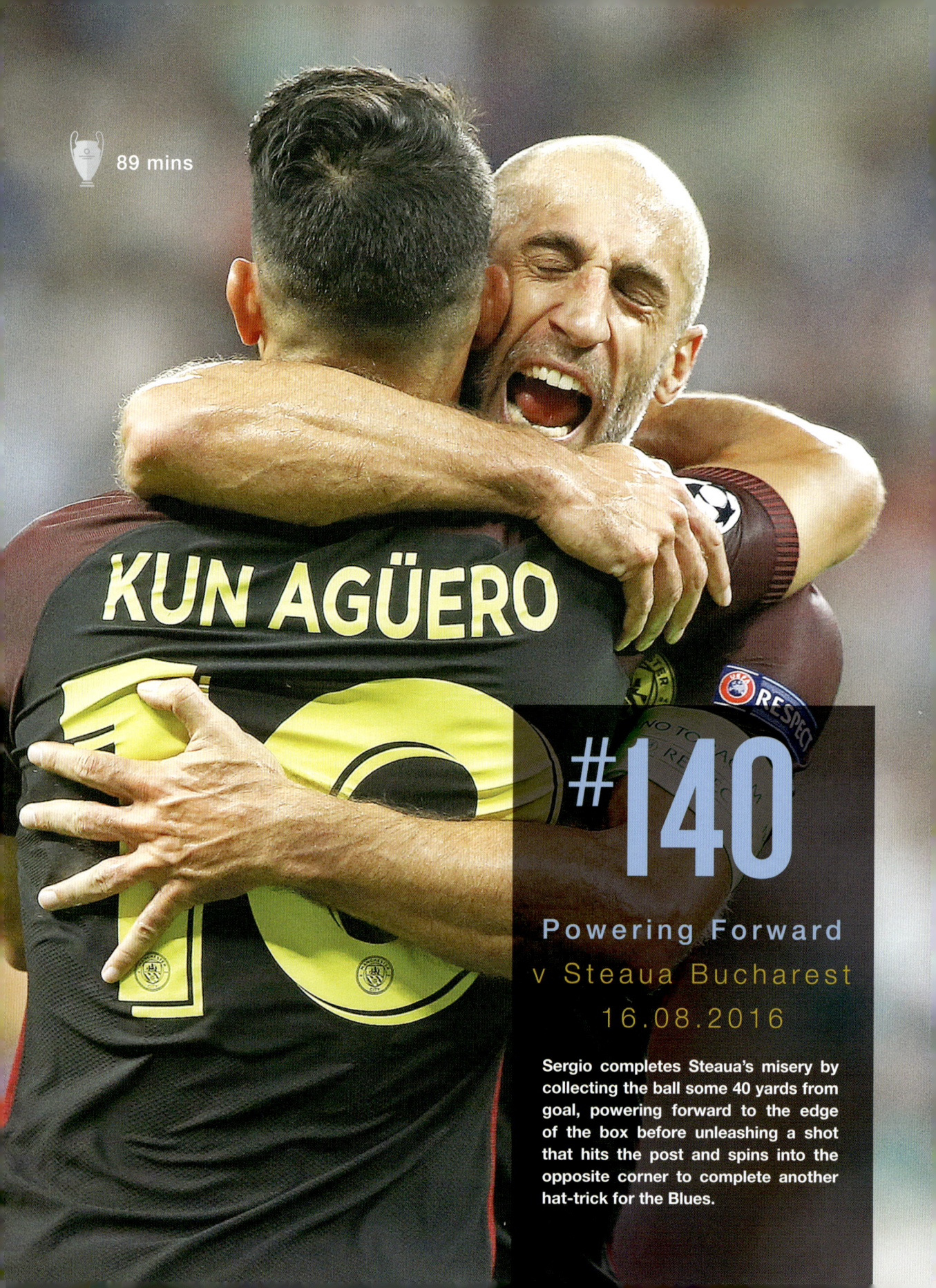

GOAL KING

27 mins

#141

Ice Cool
v Stoke City
20.08.2016

As a corner comes in, Ryan Shawcross tugs Nicolas Otamendi's shirt and the infringement is spotted by the referee, who duly awards a penalty. Aguero, despite missing two spot-kicks four days earlier against Steaua Bucharest in the Champions League qualifier second leg, makes no mistake with a powerful right-foot drive to the keeper's left.

36 mins

#142

Stoke It Up
v Stoke City
20.08.2016

A superb cross into the Stoke box finds the head of Sergio, who glances home from six yards out for his second of the afternoon.

AGÜERO

#143

More Hat-Trick Happiness
v Borussia Mönchengladbach
14.09.2016

The first of yet another treble comes in this Champions League group stage clash with Bundesliga side Börussia Monchengladbach as Aleks Kolarov's superb low cross is turned in at the near post by the on-fire Kun.

8 mins

GOAL KING

28 mins

#144

Teutonic Talent

v Borussia Mönchengladbach

14.09.2016

Another penalty clinically dispatched by Aguero after Ilkay Gundogan is fouled inside the box.

AGÜERO

GOAL KING

77 mins

#145

Just Unstoppable
v Borussia Mönchengladbach
14.09.2016

Aguero completes his hat-trick by chasing on to a clever Raheem Sterling pass inside the full-back. Drawing the keeper off his line, he nudges the ball to the left and rolls it home.

AGÜERO

9 mins

#146

Loving The Liberty

v Swansea City

24.09.2016

Fernandinho plays the ball to the right flank for Bacary Sagna. He hits a low cross in towards Aguero who moves past a defender with his first touch then fires a low shot through the legs of Swansea keeper Lukasz Fabianski from the corner of the six-yard box.

GOAL KING

#147

Fabianski Beaten Again
v Swansea City
24.09.2016

After Kevin De Bruyne is fouled inside the Swansea box, Aguero is given the chance to score his 11th goal of a season that is yet to complete September. With a variation of his usual technique, Kun chips the ball down the middle and Fabianski is easily beaten.

65 mins

AGÜERO

#148

Finding The Target
v West Bromwich Albion
29.10.2016

Ilkay Gundogan powers towards the West Brom box before playing a pass into Aguero's darting run, and the City striker makes no mistake with a powerful low drive past the keeper from the right.

19 mins

GOAL KING

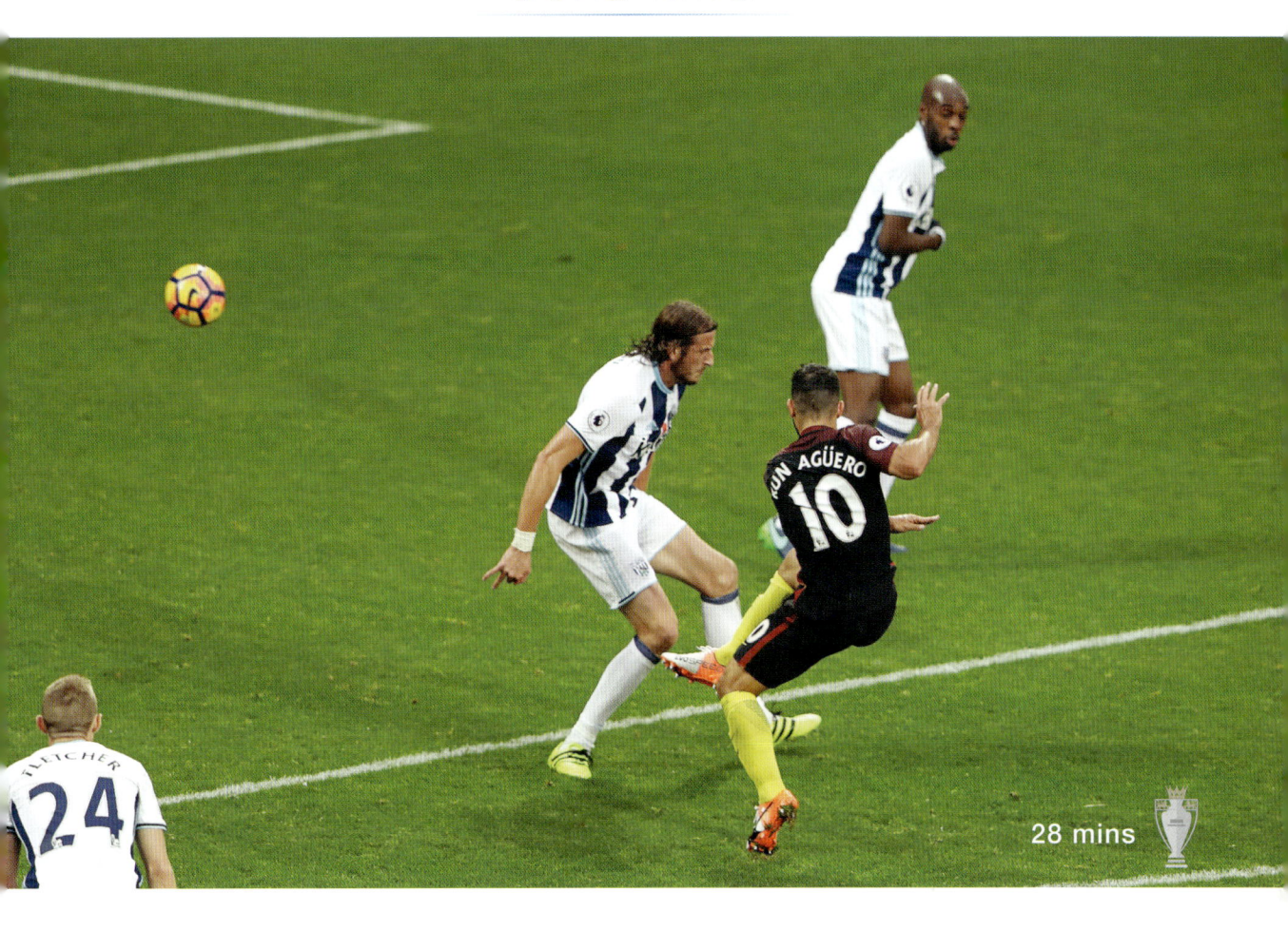

28 mins

#149

Wrestle-mania

v West Bromwich Albion

29.10.2016

When he's at his best, he's unstoppable as this howitzer of a shot proves, almost wrestling the ball off David Silva before hitting a beautiful curling shot into the top-right corner.

AGÜERO

#150

Another Landmark Goal
v Middlesbrough
05.11.2016

Sergio's landmark 150th goal for the Blues comes from close range as he turns in Kevin De Bruyne's superb cross from the right on an otherwise frustrating afternoon for the Blues, who are denied a win in the dying seconds against Boro.

43 mins

GOAL KING

#151

Close Range
v Burnley   26.11.2016

One of Sergio's scrappiest goals for City, a scramble in the six-yard box from a corner sees Nicolas Otamendi divert the ball into Kun's path, and he stabs home a goal from two yards out.

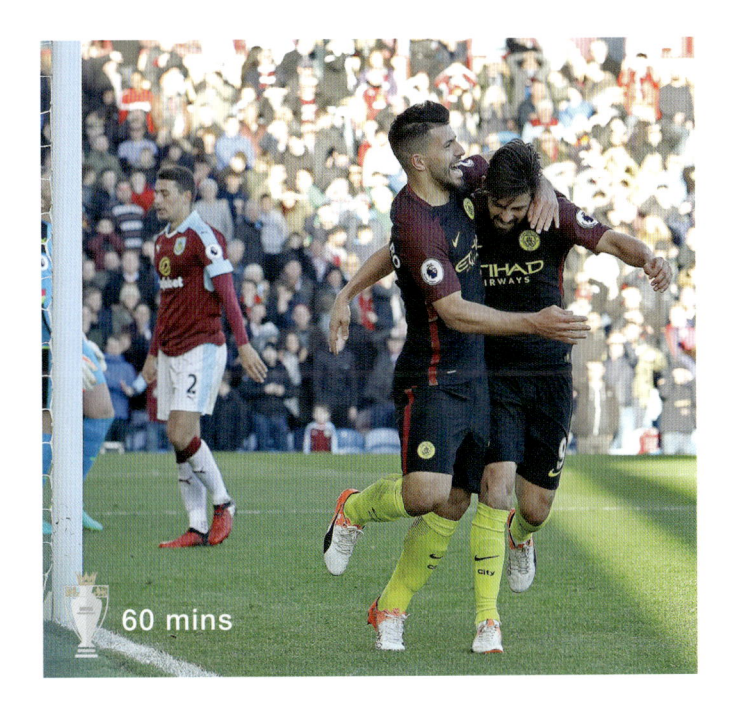

#152

Scrappy But Vital
v Burnley
26.11.2016

Another scrappy goal at Turf Moor but a vital one, nonetheless. It is great work from Fernandinho who reaches a ball that looks to be heading out before sliding a low cross into the six-yard box, where Aguero gleefully pokes home.

#153

Plaguing The Clarets

v Burnley
02.01.2017

A third successive goal against Burnley – but not the completion of a hat-trick, as these quick turnaround fixtures see the Clarets at the Etihad at the start of the New Year. If his first two against Burnley had been untidy, this was anything but as Raheem Sterling is felled in the box by goalkeeper Tom Heaton, Sergio carries on towards the loose ball before hitting a powerful shot from a tight angle past two defenders on the line and into the net. A super strike.

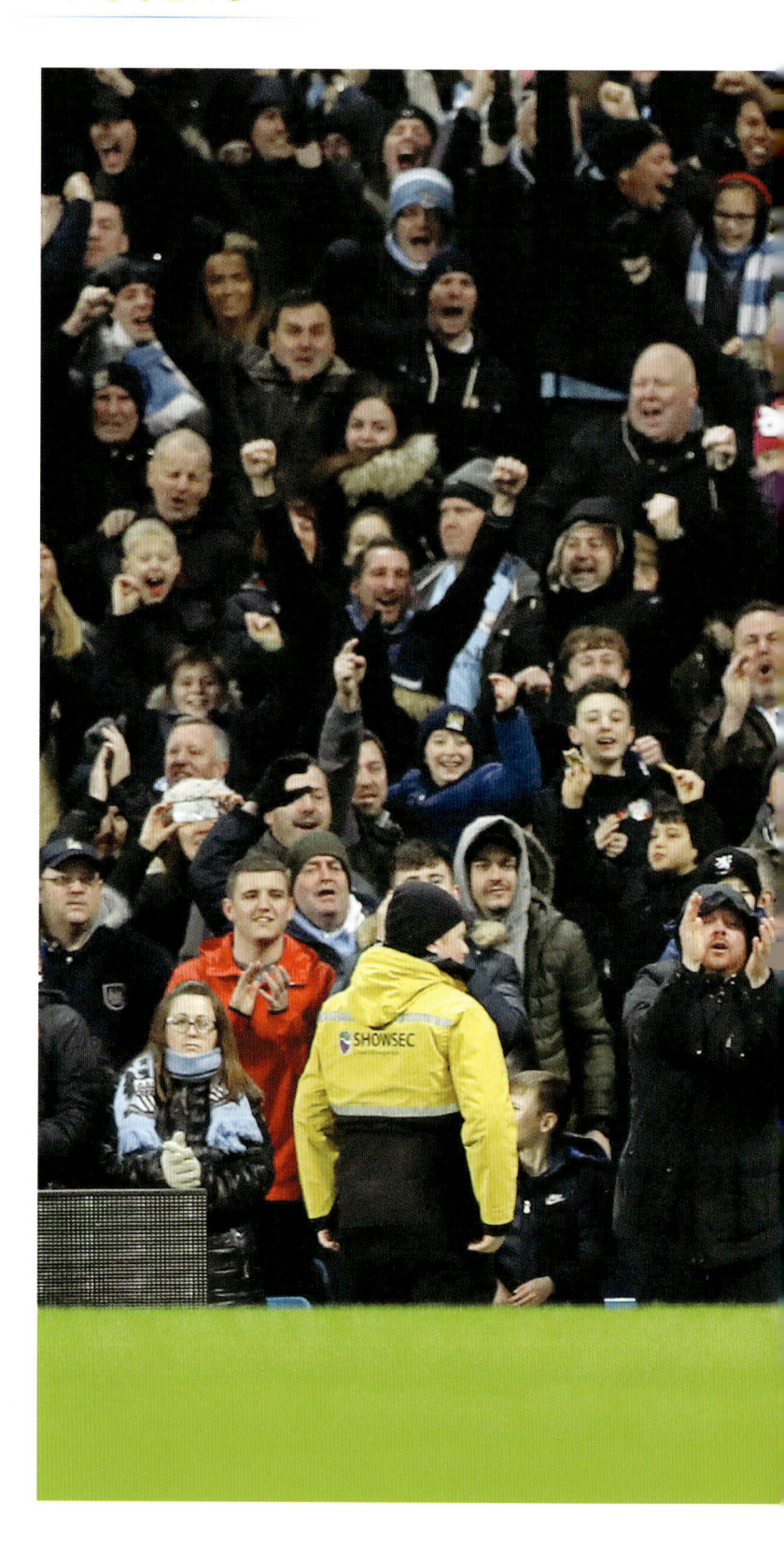

GOAL KING

62 mins

AGÜERO

50 mins

#154

London Calling
v West Ham United
06.01.2017

Raheem Sterling darts into the box on the left, checks back, spots Yaya Toure on the edge of the box and his shot is flicked home via the post by Sergio on the edge of the six-yard box for his first goal at the London Stadium.

GOAL KING

#155

Monaco Mistake
v AS Monaco
21.02.2017

Raheem Sterling spots Aguero's run, plays it into his path and Kun hits a low shot that the Monaco keeper makes a terrible hash of and the ball ends up in the back of the net.

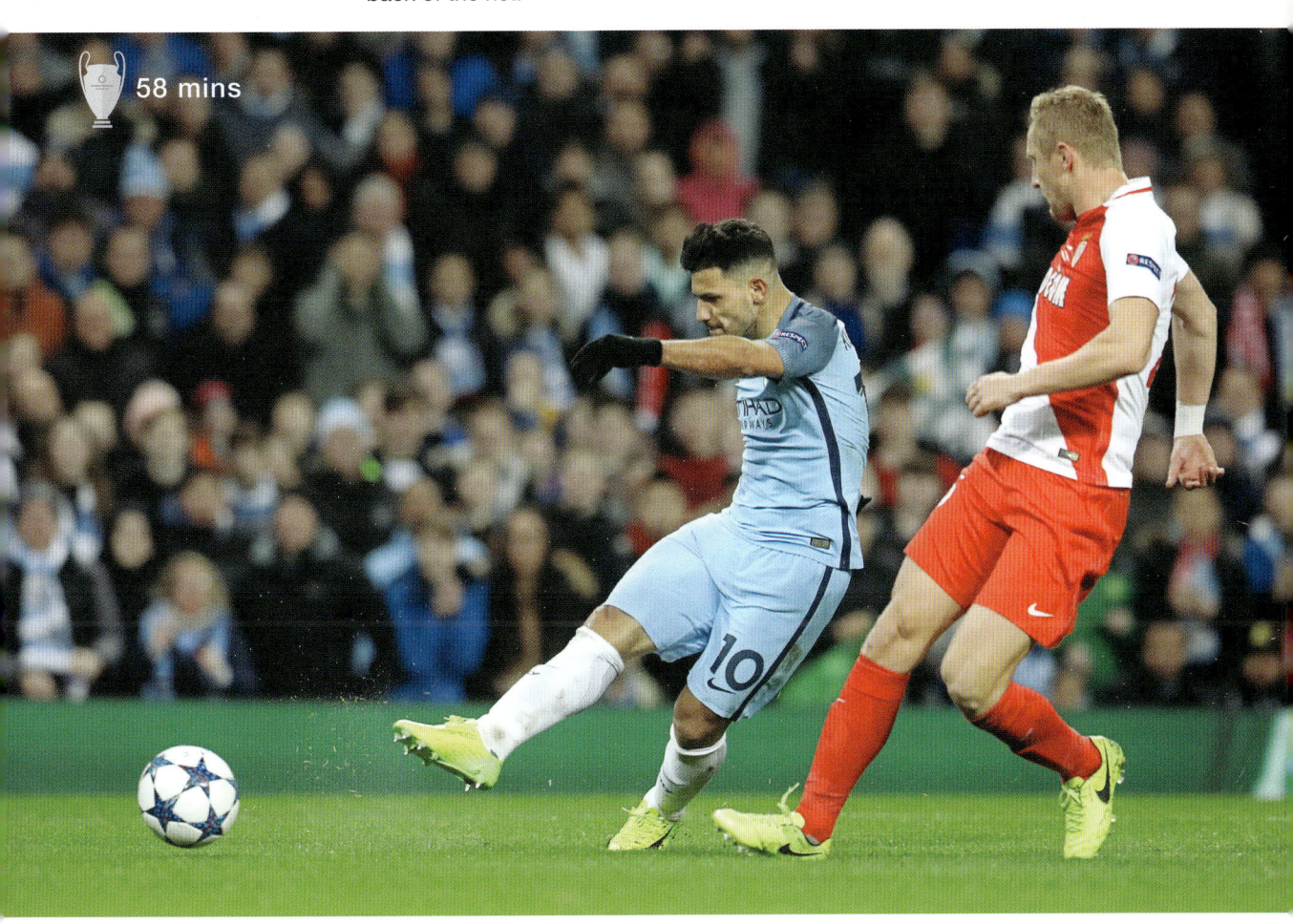

58 mins

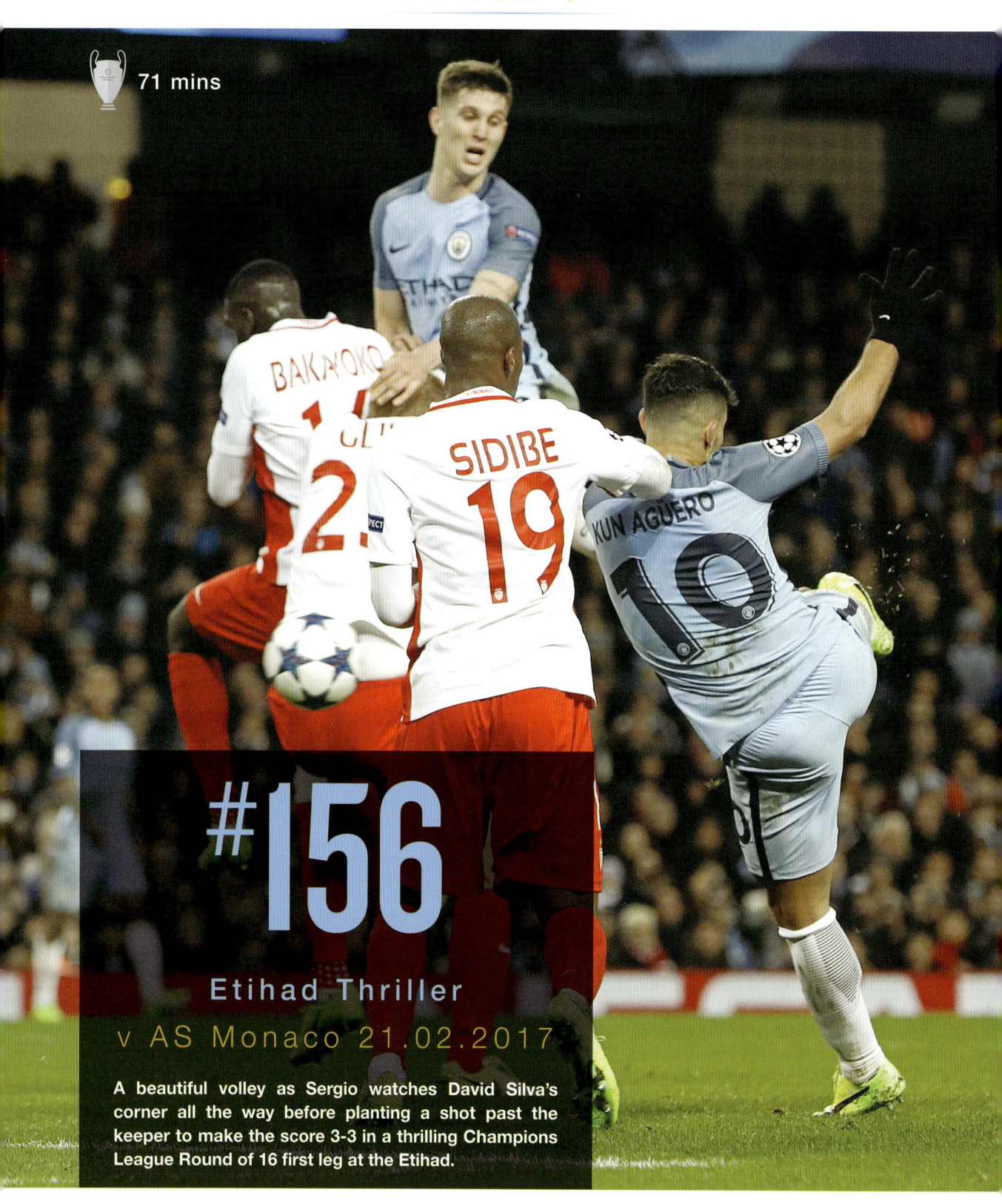

AGÜERO

71 mins

#156

Etihad Thriller

v AS Monaco 21.02.2017

A beautiful volley as Sergio watches David Silva's corner all the way before planting a shot past the keeper to make the score 3-3 in a thrilling Champions League Round of 16 first leg at the Etihad.

GOAL KING

#157

Making Sure
v Huddersfield Town
01.03.2017

Sergio sends a penalty powerfully past the keeper after Nicolas Otamendi had been fouled in the box.

AGÜERO

73 mins

GOAL KING

#158

First To React
v Huddersfield Town
01.03.2017

Raheem Sterling sends a ball towards the six-yard box from the right and Sergio is on to it like a flash, turning the ball home with a low shot from the right.

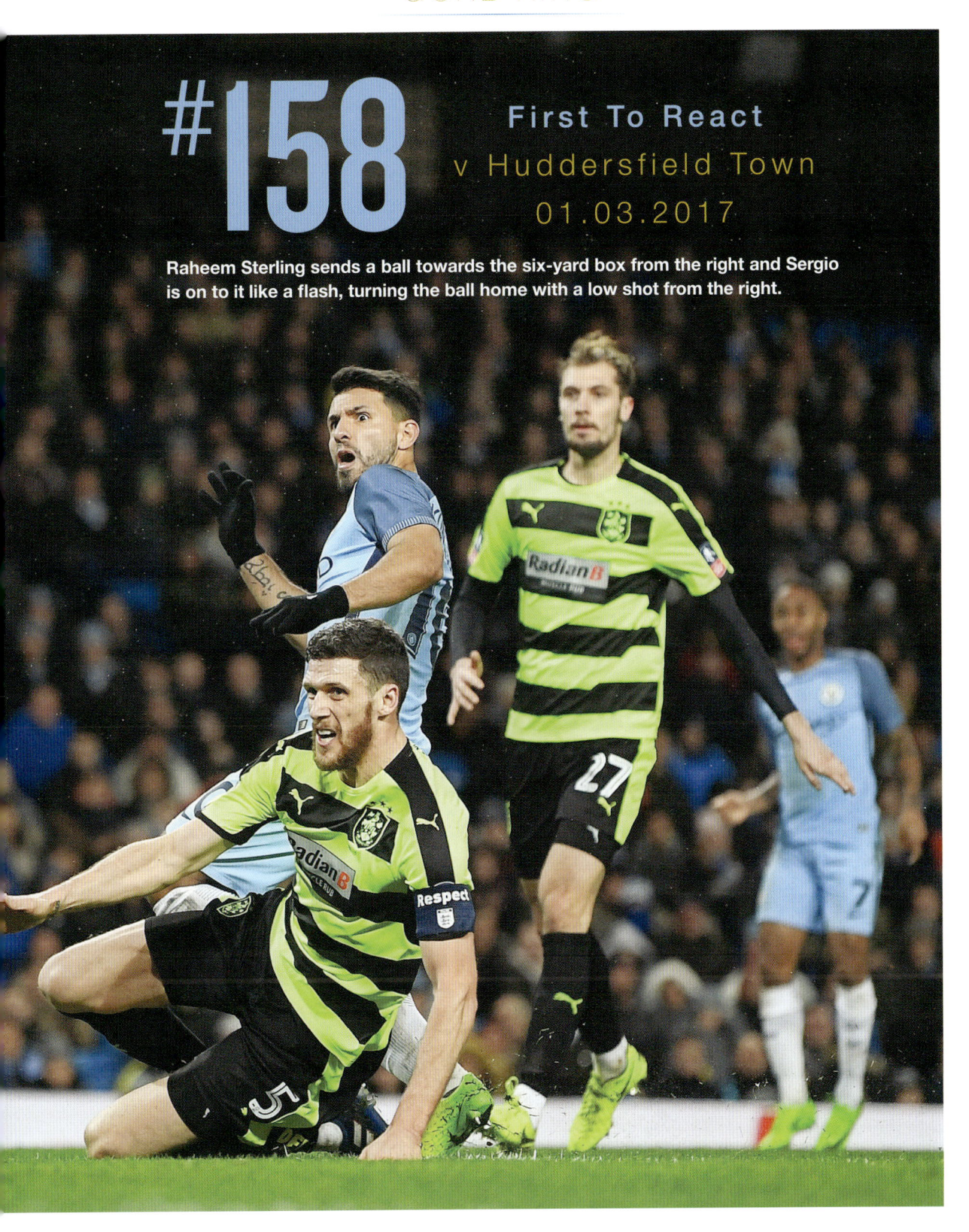

AGÜERO

42 mins

#159

Sterling Work

v Sunderland

05.03.2017

Another assist by Raheem Sterling as his understanding of Sergio's movement brings yet more reward. Sterling's clever low pass into the six-yard box allows Aguero to nip in between two defenders before dinking the ball past the keeper.

GOAL KING

#160

Boro Beaten
v Middlesbrough
11.03.2017

Leroy Sane dashes down the right flank, looks up and then whips the perfect low cross into the six-yard box where Aguero is most lethal and he makes no mistake with a smart finish from five yards out.

67 mins

69 mins

#161

Fox In The Box
v Liverpool   19.03.2017

A goal so typical of Sergio Aguero. Kevin De Bruyne's excellent low cross to the edge of the six-yard box is swept home by Aguero's right boot with precision.

AGÜERO

42 mins

#162

Restoring The Lead
v Arsenal 02.04.2017

Having just conceded at the other end to make it 1-1, the Blues regain the lead with the tried and trusted partnership of David Silva and Sergio as the Spaniard slips a ball into the box to Kun who, from a tight angle, buries a low shot past David Ospina to score.

GOAL KING

26 mins

#163

The Equaliser
v Chelsea 05.04.2017

David Silva sees his shot well saved by Thibaut Courtois at the near post, but the Belgian keeper can only push the ball out to the edge of the six-yard box where Aguero is waiting to pounce quicker than anyone else to level the scores at Stamford Bridge against champions-elect Chelsea.

AGÜERO

48 mins

#164

From One To 11

v Hull City

08.04.2017

This goal is a superb team passing move that involves all City's players and ends when Raheem Sterling darts into the box and slides a low ball across the face of goal for Aguero to just about bundle over the line – typically, he looks unhappy at his finish!

GOAL KING

#165

De Bruyne Brilliance
v Southampton
15.04.2017

With City in the middle of a rampant period of play, Kevin De Bruyne somehow digs a superb cross in from the right of the Southampton box and Aguero wants it more than the home defenders as he heads home from close range to put the Blues 3-0 up at St Mary's.

80 mins

AGÜERO

62 mins

GOAL KING

#166

Wembley Woes
v Arsenal
23.04.2017

Yaya Toure's long pass into the Arsenal half is controlled by Aguero who speeds away from defender Nacho Monreal. He pushes the ball towards goal and as Petr Cech advances he calmly lifts it over the Gunners' keeper to put City ahead in this FA Cup semi-final at Wembley. It's just reward for Kun who had a perfectly good goal wiped out in the first half when the assistant referee wrongly deemed Leroy Sane's cross to have curled out of play momentarily. The Blues, however, let the lead slip and eventually lose 2-1.

AGÜERO

69 mins

#167

Stepping Up
v Middlesbrough
30.04.2017

Sergio knocks home another penalty with consummate ease after Leroy Sane was adjudged to have been fouled in the box.

GOAL KING

AGÜERO

23 mins

#168

Within Sight

v Watford

21.05.2017

The first of two goals at Vicarage Road for Sergio comes after a measured through ball from Kevin De Bruyne sets Kun clear, and his low shot to the left of the keeper gives the Blues the lead.

GOAL KING

#169

A Maturing Master
v Watford 21.05.2017

Leroy Sane's dash past a static Watford defence to the bye-line sees the German winger pull the ball back into the path of Aguero, who sweeps the ball home from close range for his 33rd of the campaign – his best-ever seasonal tally and proof that, if anything, he is getting better as he gets older!

36 mins

2017/18

SEASON

"I'm very happy to break the record. If I can keep scoring goals for City - even better - but winning is the most important thing..."

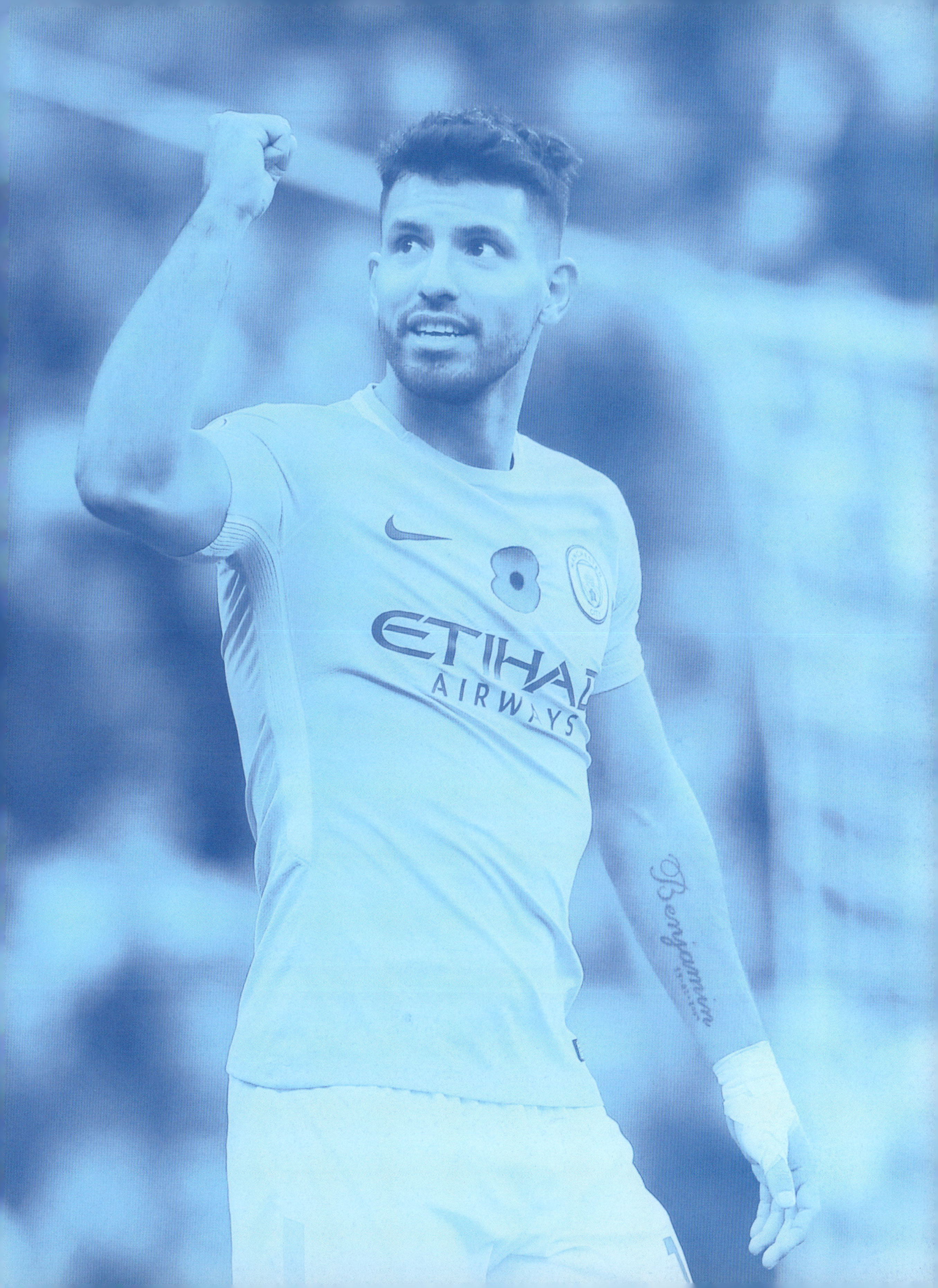
AIRWAYS

AGÜERO

70 mins

#170

Patience Pays Off

v Brighton & Hove Albion

12.08.2017

City have to be patient against Premier League newcomers Brighton, who are buoyed by a passionate home crowd at the Amex Stadium. The Blues finally make the breakthrough as David Silva slots a ball into Aguero in the box and his powerful shot across the keeper puts City in command at last.

24 mins

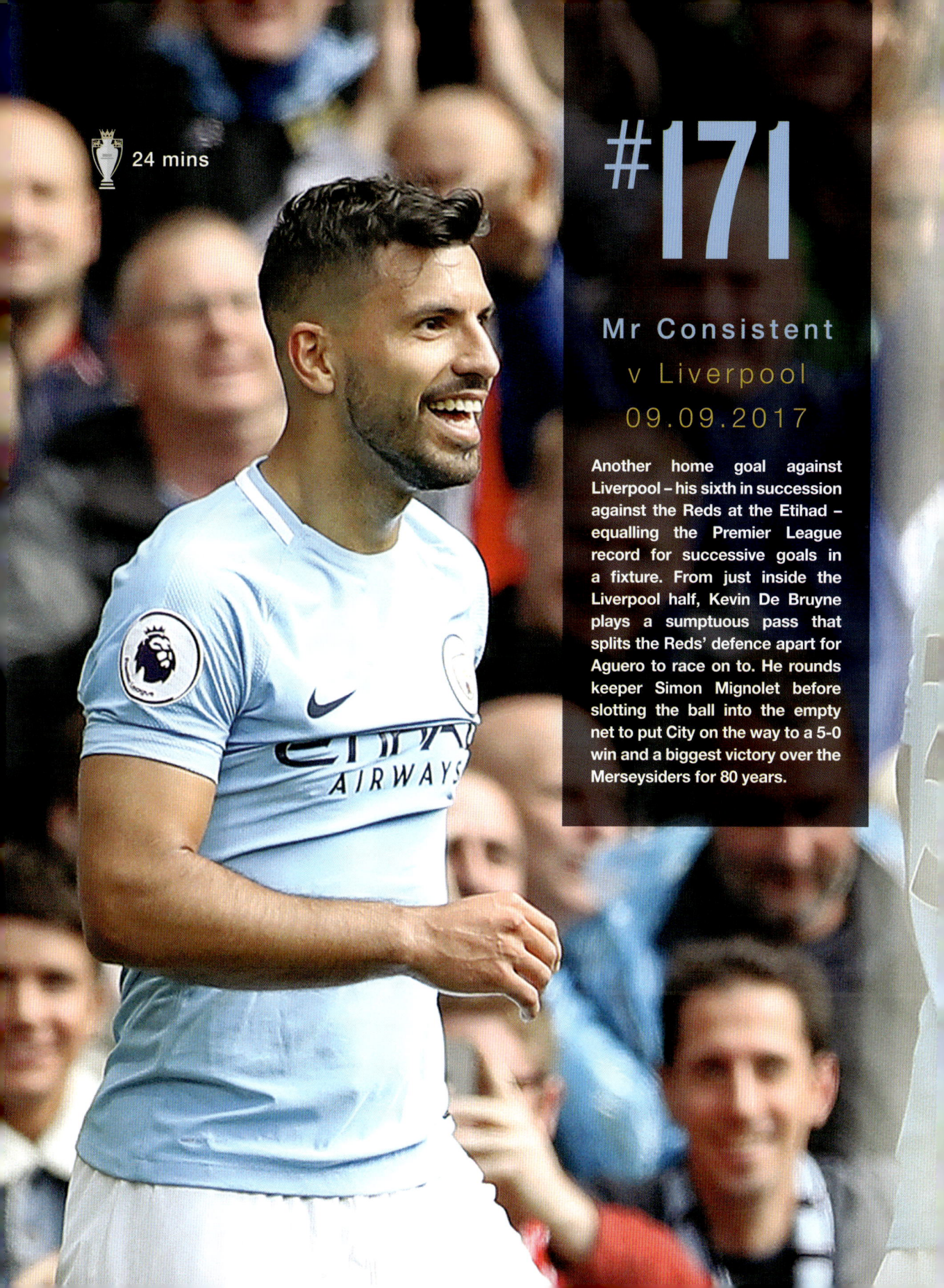

#171

Mr Consistent
v Liverpool
09.09.2017

Another home goal against Liverpool – his sixth in succession against the Reds at the Etihad – equalling the Premier League record for successive goals in a fixture. From just inside the Liverpool half, Kevin De Bruyne plays a sumptuous pass that splits the Reds' defence apart for Aguero to race on to. He rounds keeper Simon Mignolet before slotting the ball into the empty net to put City on the way to a 5-0 win and a biggest victory over the Merseysiders for 80 years.

AGÜERO

10 mins

#172

Walker Lends A Hand
v Feyenoord
13.09.2017

A great burst down the right flank by Kyle Walker sees the England defender spot Aguero's run towards the six-yard box, and his low cross is turned in expertly from close range by the Argentine.

GOAL KING

#173

Hornets Stung
v Watford
16.09.2017

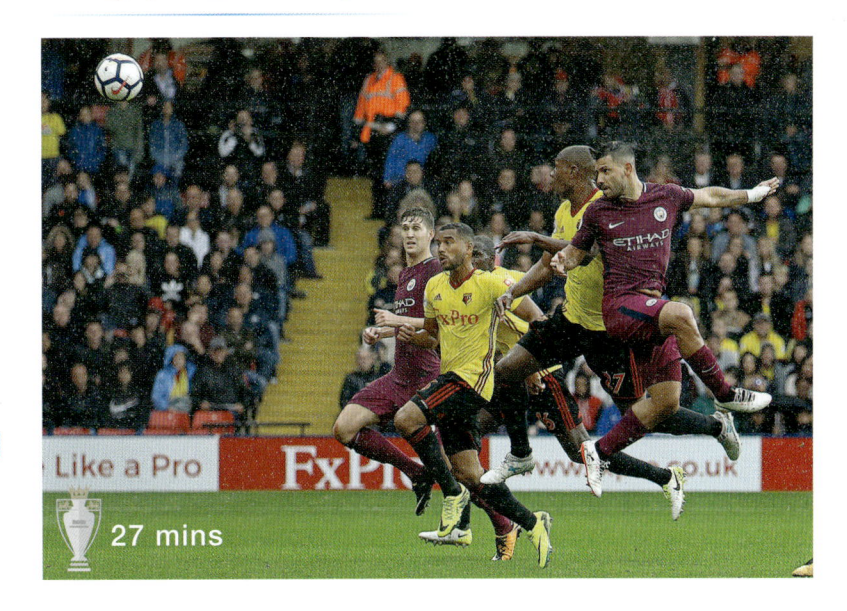

27 mins

The first of yet another hat-trick and his second career treble against the Hornets. Kevin De Bruyne's superb free-kick into the box is begging to be headed by someone and – of course – Sergio is first to arrive, planting a firm header to Heurelho Gomes' right.

31 mins

#174

They Keep Coming
v Watford
16.09.2017

A second in four minutes for Sergio as David Silva's clever early pass catches the Watford defence cold and it's an easy tap-in for Kun at the far post.

AGÜERO

81 mins

GOAL KING

#175

Another Match Ball
v Watford
16.09.2017

One of his best for City? Definitely, maybe! Kyle Walker knocks the ball in with a short pass from the right and Aguero does the rest, gliding past one, two, three and then a fourth Watford defender before sliding his third of the game past Heurelho Gomes to complete a superb hat-trick. It is a quite breath-taking individual goal that his son Benjamin's grandfather, Diego Maradona, would be proud of!

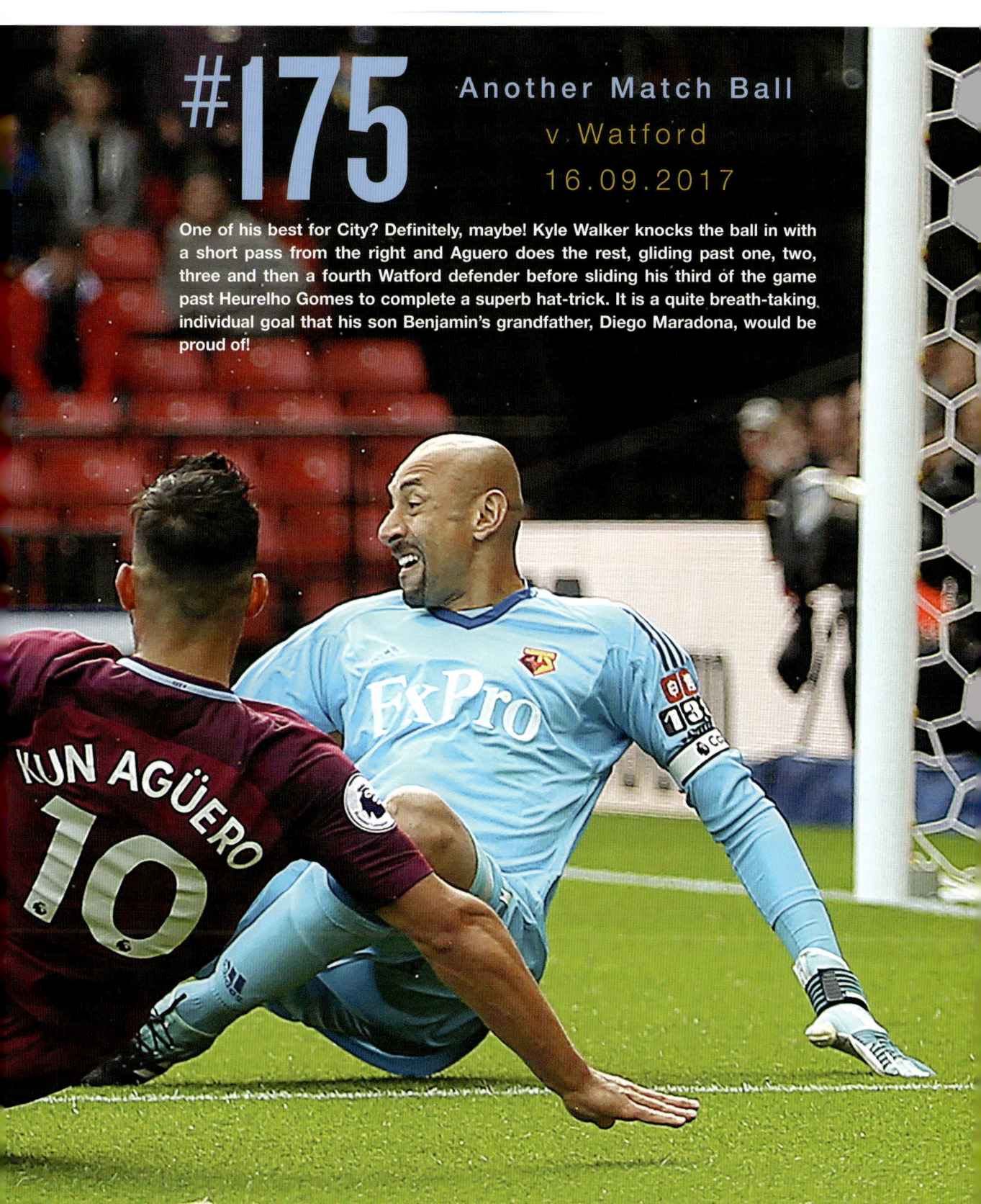

AGÜERO

79 mins

#176

Getting So Close

v Crystal Palace

23.09.2017

The goal that puts Sergio one shy of Eric Brook's record total of 177. Leroy Sane whips in a curling cross and the accuracy is such Sergio needs to only guide a header low and past the goalkeeper from seven yards out, having not had to adjust his feet at all.

GOAL KING

#177

Drawing Level
v Burnley
21.10.2017

Finally, Sergio draws level with Eric Brook as he plants home his 177th goal for the Blues. There's a whiff of controversy as Burnley argue with the referee's decision to award a penalty following Bernardo Silva's clash with Clarets keeper Nick Pope. Sergio ignores the fuss and focuses on the job in hand before calmly sending Pope the wrong way to officially write his name into the Manchester City history books as the Blues' all-time joint-top goalscorer. Now, time to set a new record…

30 mins

AGÜERO

#178

The Greatest
v Napoli
01.11.2017

The goal City fans had been waiting for. Though Sergio had scored during a penalty shoot-out against Wolves eight days earlier, it didn't count towards his record. He had to then watch the next game from the bench as an unused substitute. It seemed he'd been poised forever on the cusp of history and with more than an hour of the Champions League clash with Napoli gone, many wondered whether he'd have to wait again to replace Eric Brook at the top of City's all-time goalscorers list. Then, Fernandinho breaks out of defence and plays the perfect ball for Leroy Sane who powers through the Napoli defence on the halfway line and heads for goal. A fine last-ditch tackle foils the German winger but Sergio is first to react to the loose ball. He collects 30 yards out and heads into the box with two defenders snapping at his heels before striking a precision shot from 18 yards past Pepe Reina to give the Blues the lead. It takes Aguero past Brook's record and forever writes his name into the Club's history books. A terrific goal from a fantastic player who will now try and set the bar even higher.

69 mins

GOAL KING

THE MAN HE BEAT

Aguero overtook Eric Brook as City's greatest ever goalscorer

Eric Brook held the honour of City's greatest goalscorer for 78 years and chances are, if he could have picked somebody to have taken his mantle, it would have been Sergio Aguero.

The pair share more than a few similarities. They were both born into working-class families with little or no money, both fought their way to becoming professional footballers and each were stocky, muscular players who scored all types of goals (including many penalties) and have a powerful shot in their armoury.

Brook scored 177 goals in 491 appearances for City between 1928 and 1940 and led the scoring charts after overtaking Tom Johnson's total of 166 with a goal away to Bradford City in September 1938.

There is no doubt Brook, the son of a coalminer, was a special player and a fantastic signing for City. A left-winger by trade, Brook rarely stayed on the flank and considered the position as somewhere to find his bearings. Any right-back hoping to man-mark Brook from start-to-finish would likely leave a big hole on one side of the defence as the City 'winger' had a licence to roam – and roam he most certainly did!

As noted, Brook cut a powerful figure, was physically imposing and strong.

He possessed one of the most powerful shots of his era and would regularly thump home penalties with venom.

Though he won just 18 England caps, many believe he was one of the best players of the late 1920s and 1930s and that perhaps he didn't get the recognition he deserved.

Born in Mexborough, Yorkshire in 1907, Brook signed for Barnsley as a teenager and remained with the Tykes for three years before City came in with an offer of £6,000 for Brook and his team-mate Fred Tilson in March 1928 – an inspired move by manager Peter Hodge, with Tilson's 132 career goals for the Blues meaning the pair would net an incredible 310 goals between them in a combined appearance total of 726 matches – not bad value for money!

Brook and Tilson joined Tom Johnson, Billy Austin and Frank Roberts to form one of the most lethal forward lines in English football and though he only made 12 starts, Brook played his part as the Blues won promotion from Division Two.

Brook quickly became integral in City's side, scoring 14 goals in 42 league appearances during his first full campaign at Maine Road

ERIC BROOK

and achieved double figures in goals during his first five seasons, rarely missing a game.

But for Arsenal's Cliff Bastin, he would likely have doubled his appearances for England, but the pair were considered too similar in their style and only played in the same side a few times.

City lifted the FA Cup in 1934, with Brook assisting the winning goal for Tilson, and were crowned champions of England in 1937. Brook rarely missed a game in either campaign and scored twice in the 4-1 win over Sheffield Wednesday at Maine Road to clinch the title, watched by a crowd of more than 55,000.

Maybe only as City could back then, the Blues outscored every other side in the top flight but were relegated as defending champions – the only time this has ever happened in English football – and the 1938/39 campaign in Division Two would be Brook's last full season for the Blues.

He played three games of the 1939/40 season before World War 2 meant the league was suspended and the one goal he scored that 'season' was scrubbed from the record books. Though he made a handful of wartime appearances in 1939, a car crash left him with a fractured skull and, unable to head the ball again, he retired at the relatively young age of 32.

Unable to resume his career as many of his peers did after the war, Brook instead found other employment outside of football, working as a coach driver, pub landlord in Halifax and even a crane operator before passing away aged just 57 at his home in Wythenshawe.

At the time, Brook has been somewhat forgotten by football and his achievements consigned to the history books.

How fitting, then, that the name of Eric Brook is once again being talked and written about by the football world – and who better to wrestle the mantle of greatest Manchester City goalscorer than Sergio Aguero?

SERGIO AGÜERO

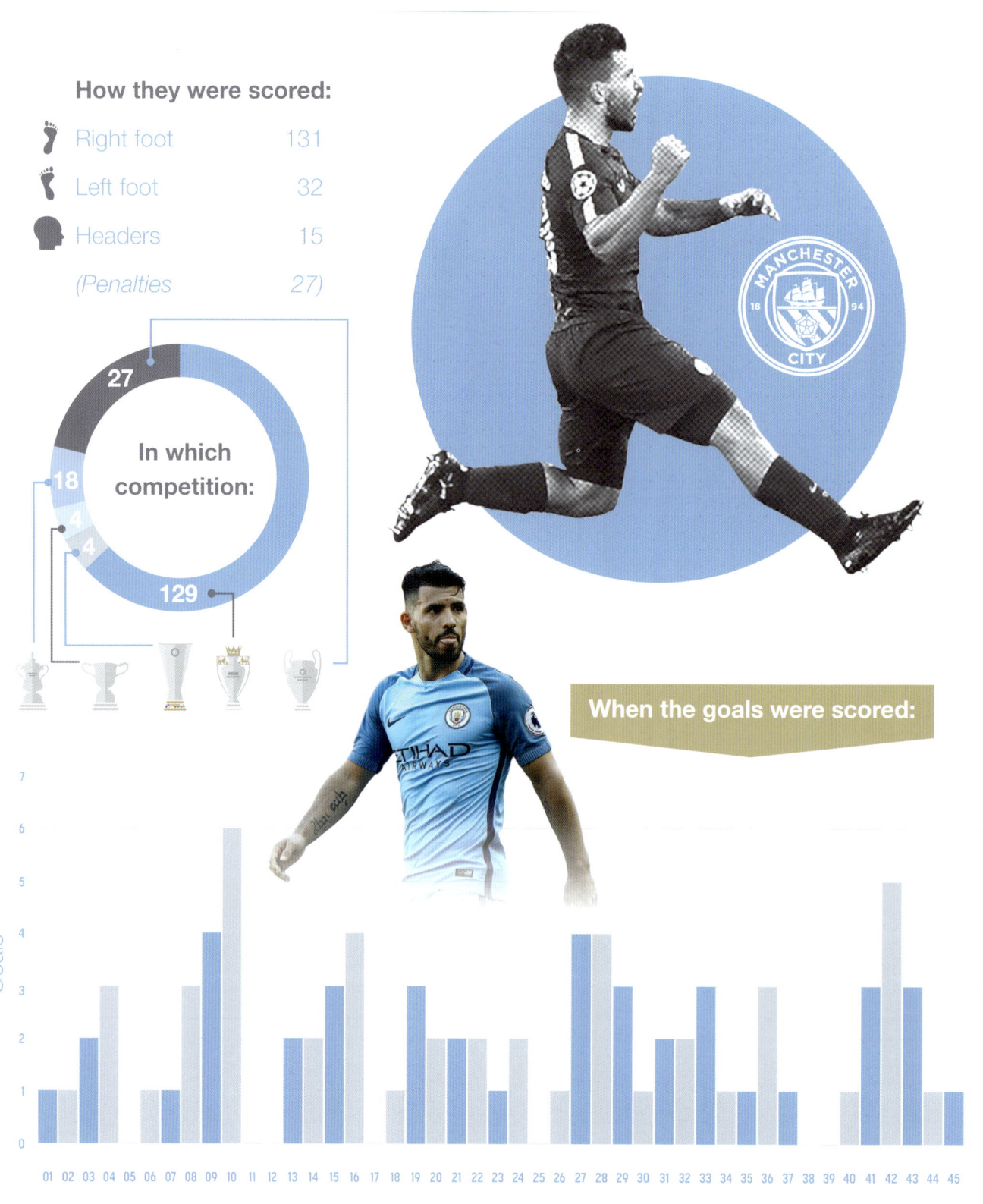

How they were scored:

- Right foot — 131
- Left foot — 32
- Headers — 15
- (Penalties — 27)

In which competition:
- 27
- 18
- 4
- 4
- 129

When the goals were scored:

Goals / Minutes (01–45)

STATISTICS

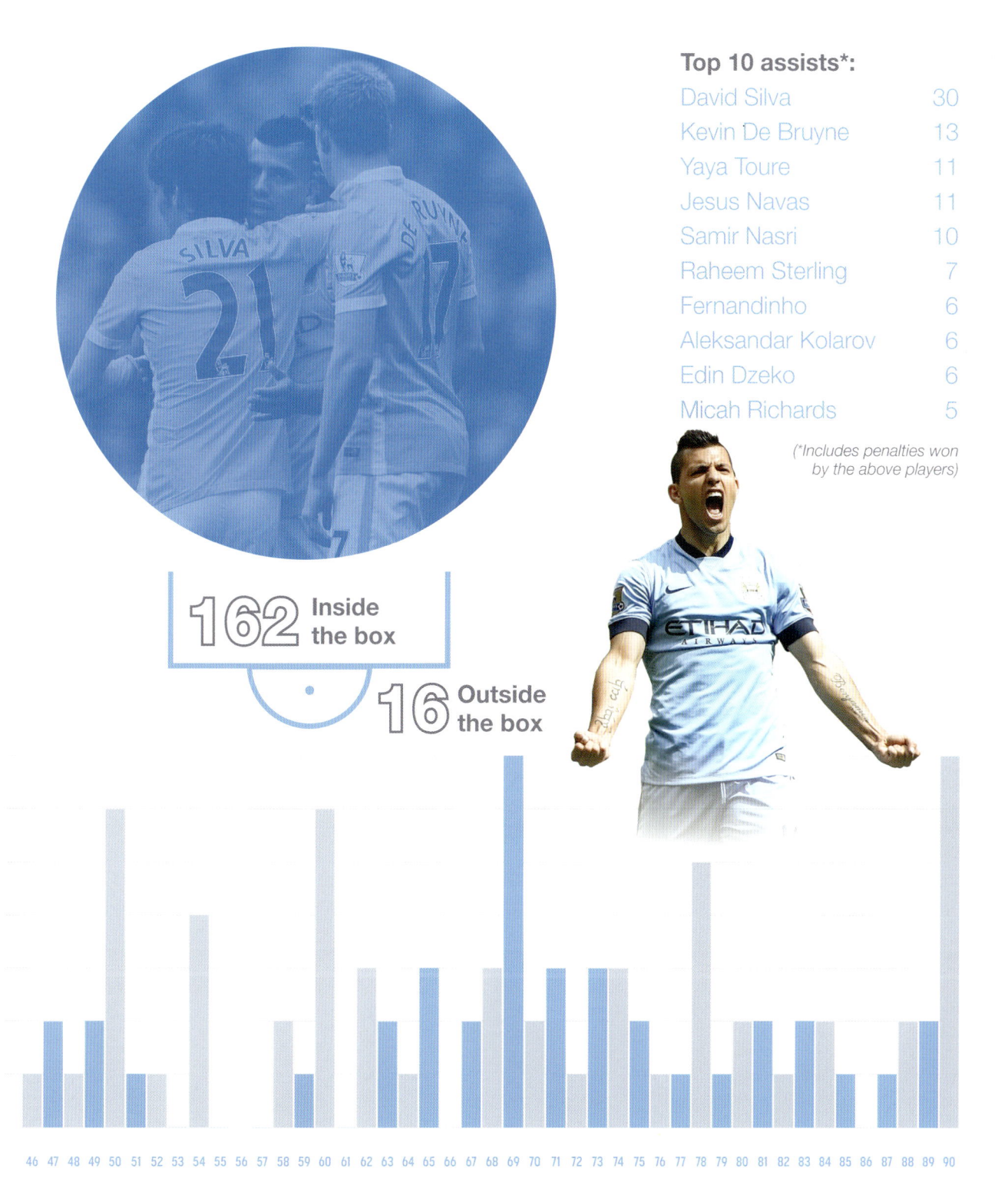

Top 10 assists*:

David Silva	30
Kevin De Bruyne	13
Yaya Toure	11
Jesus Navas	11
Samir Nasri	10
Raheem Sterling	7
Fernandinho	6
Aleksandar Kolarov	6
Edin Dzeko	6
Micah Richards	5

*(*Includes penalties won by the above players)*

162 Inside the box

16 Outside the box

Minutes

AGÜERO
GOAL KING